College COMPOSITION

CLEP* Test Study Guide

All rights reserved. This Study Guide, Book and Flashcards are protected under the US Copyright Law. No part of this book or study guide or flashcards may be reproduced, distributed or stored in a retrieval system, or transmitted in any form or by any means, electronic, mechanical, photocopying, recording, or otherwise, without the prior written permission of the publisher Breely Crush Publishing, LLC.

© 2020 Breely Crush Publishing, LLC

*CLEP is a registered trademark of the College Entrance Examination Board which does not endorse this book.

971010420143

Copyright ©2003 - 2020, Breely Crush Publishing, LLC.

All rights reserved.

This Study Guide, Book and Flashcards are protected under the US Copyright Law. No part of this publication may be reproduced, distributed or stored in a retrieval system, or transmitted in any form or by any means, electronic, mechanical, photocopying, recording, or otherwise, without the prior written permission of the publisher Breely Crush Publishing, LLC.

Published by Breely Crush Publishing, LLC
10808 River Front Parkway
South Jordan, UT 84095
www.breelycrushpublishing.com

ISBN-10: 1-61433-630-X
ISBN-13: 978-1-61433-630-3

Printed and bound in the United States of America.

*CLEP is a registered trademark of the College Entrance Examination Board which does not endorse this book.

Table of Contents

Part I: Beginning with Correct Grammar 1
    I. Introduction 1
    II. Syntax 1
    III. Sentence Boundaries 2
    IV. Correct Sentences 5
Sample Test Questions 6
    V. Sentence Variety 7
    VI. Agreement 8
    VII. Correct Idiom 10
    VIII. Active Voice 11
    IX. Logical Comparisons 11
    X. Punctuation 12
Sample Test Questions 14
Part II: Ability to Recognize Logical Development 18
    I. Organization 18
    II. Evaluation of Evidence 19
    III. Awareness of Audience Tone and Purpose 19
    IV. Level of Detail 20
    V. Consistency of Topic Focus 20
    VI. Sentence Variety 21
    VII. Paragraph Coherence 21
    VIII. Main Idea / Thesis Statements 22
    IX. Rhetorical Effects and Emphasis 22
    X. Use of Language 23
    XI. Evaluation of Author's Authority and Appeal 24
    XII. Evaluation of Reasoning 25
    XIII. Shift in Point of View 26
    XIV. 5 X 5 Paragraph Essay 26
    XV. Sentence Variety 26
    Comparisons 27
Sample Test Questions 29
Part III: Ability to Use Resource Materials 38
    I. Evaluating Sources 38
    II. Integrating Research Material Into the Paper 39
    III. Manuscript Format and Documentation 41
    IV. Reference Skills 44
    V. Use of Reference Books 45
    VI. Footnotes and Endnotes 46
Sample Test Questions 49

Essay Writing *51*
Strategy for Writing the Entire Essay *52*
       Strategy for Writing Each Paragraph *53*
Practice Essay Topics *54*
Additional Practice Questions *55*
   I. Punctuation *55*
   II. Combined Sentences *56*
   III. Possessives *57*
   IV. Subordination and Coordination *59*
   V. Identifying Sentence Errors *60*
   VI. Improving Sentences *61*
   VII. The Following is a Draft of a Student Composition
       with the Sentences Numbered for Reference *63*
   VIII. The Following is a Paragraph from the Draft of a
       Student Composition with the Sentences Numbered for Reference *65*
   IX. Word Choice and Idiom *66*
   X. Verb Forms *68*
Answer Key *69*
Additional Sample Test Questions *70*
Answer Key *85*
Test Taking Strategies *86*
What Your Score Means *86*
Test Preparation *87*
Legal Note *87*

 Part I: Beginning with Correct Grammar

I. *Introduction*

You may have heard stories about those terrible English Professors who take sadistic joy in bleeding red ink on your compositions. You may even have heard tales about students who made A's in high school and royally fail their first college paper. Maybe you've just imagined horror and mayhem in those hallowed halls – all caused by vindictive teachers who have impossible rules.

Don't erase your papers in frustration. Just erase your mind of those misconceptions and fears. English teachers are not evil, nor do they grade papers based on intangible ideas in their own heads. The fundamentals of good writing are not based on opinion; they are based on concrete rules and solid guidelines that you CAN master. No one is born a great writer, but everyone can learn the rules and become skilled and competent in language use.

II. *Syntax*

Don't let the word scare you. "Syntax" is a fancy term that simply means how words are put together. Your understanding of syntax is encapsulated in your brain from the time you learned how to talk, but a few small "polishing points" could improve your writing.

Parallelism: Think of parallel bars or parallel lines. Both are images that look just like each other. That's exactly what it means in language as well. Whenever you have three items in a series, they must all be alike, and NOT like the following sentence where the third verb doesn't match the first two.

"The young girl skipped, laughed, and was singing a limerick as she went down the street."

Since parallelism means that all the items in a series look the same, the third verb must be put into the simple past tense.

"The young girl skipped, laughed, and sang a limerick as she went down the street."

Another type of parallelism is comparing two items for emphasis. One of the most famous examples is Patrick Henry's line, "Give me liberty, or give me death." If he had uttered, "Give me liberty or death," the statement would never have gone down in history as a great moment of oratory. The use of parallel structure made it work.

Coordination: Coordination is the term that refers to how you connect ideas together. When you connect two sentences with a comma and one of the seven conjunctions (for, and, nor, but, or, yet, so), then you are basically giving each of the ideas equal importance.

"The house was huge, and it was expensive."

Subordination: Subordination is a term similar to coordination because it refers to how you put ideas together, but instead of making the ideas equal in importance, subordination makes one idea "subordinate" to the other. The idea with more weight is placed in the independent clause. The less important idea is then placed in a dependent clause.

"Even though the ring didn't cost much, it was my most treasured possession."

Modifiers: A "modifier" is simply a descriptive phrase or word. A "misplaced modifier" happens when a descriptive phrase is placed next to a noun, but it's not the noun it's supposed to describe.

As a young girl, Bobby walked me to school.

Notice that the descriptive phrase is placed next to the noun Bobby. Now, wouldn't Bobby be horrified to think that he was once a young girl?

The simplest cure for a misplaced modifier is to make sure that the descriptive phrase is placed nearest the noun which it modifies.

As a young girl, I often found Bobby walking me to school OR
As a young man, Bobby often walked me to school.

III. Sentence Boundaries

The first thing you have to do is make sure you understand how to craft a grammatically correct sentence.

The Comma Splice

Probably the most common error in College Composition, a comma splice occurs when two complete sentences are fused together with a comma. Just remember this: a comma can NEVER, EVER, hold two complete sentences together by itself.

No matter where you go to school or who your teacher is, it will always be WRONG to write any of the following sentences:

I can't go to school today, I will go tomorrow.
The dog just ran into the street, he was running when he was hit by a car.
Eat your sandwich, then take a bath.

Each phrase of the above sentences is a complete idea with a subject, a verb, and a sense of completeness. Each half of the sentence would stand by itself. Since you can NEVER, EVER hold two complete sentences together with a comma, you see that all of the above sentences are incorrect.

<u>There are multiple ways of fixing a comma splice</u>:

1) Put a period in between the two sentences. "I can't go to school today. I will go tomorrow."

2) Use a comma with one of these words: for, and, nor, but, or, yet, so. These seven words are called conjunctions. If you want to use a comma between the two sentences, you must also use a conjunction. You can't have one without the other and be right. Think of it as a kind of epoxy glue which requires two types of adhesive to work.

   Tip: Memorize the seven conjunctions. Remember that the word "then" is NOT a conjunction, and so you must add in one of the necessary seven words:

   "Eat your sandwich, and then take a bath."

3) Use a semicolon to attach two sentences together. A semicolon is used to connect two sentences that are closely related in meaning. In general, use a semicolon in the same place as you would a period. Example: "The dog just ran into the street; he was running when he was hit by a car."

4) Use a semicolon to attach two sentences together with a word known as a conjunctive adverb, words like however, therefore, subsequently, consequently, moreover, also, certainly, in addition, otherwise. "I can't go to school today; however, I will go tomorrow."

<u>The Fused or Run-On Sentence</u>: The "run-on" or fused sentence is simply two sentences put together without appropriate punctuation in between. If there are two parts to a sentence and both parts can stand alone, there must be appropriate "breaking" apart of the sentences. The following example illustrates this error.

"Love means many different things to many people it's hard to give a distinct definition of it."

Notice that the above word grouping contains TWO subjects and TWO verbs: "Love means many different things to many people / "It is hard to give a distinct definition of it." Each word grouping has a subject, a verb, and a sense of completeness, so they cannot be lumped into one sentence without punctuation.

How to fix run-on sentences:

1) The easiest way to fix a run-on sentence is to break it up into two sentences. You may also use some of the same repair strategies that you use for comma splices.
2) Utilize a semicolon in between the two independent clauses.
3) Utilize a semicolon AND a conjunctive adverb between the two independent clauses.
4) Insert a comma and a conjunction between the two word groups.
5) Make one of the phrases a DEPENDENT clause so that it has to rely on the other clause to make it a complete sentence:

   For example: "Since love means many different things to many people, it's hard to give a distinct definition of it."

The Sentence Fragment

A "fragment" is incomplete. It is a word grouping that lacks a subject, a verb, or a sense of completeness.

"I know he didn't commit the crime. Because he was at the movies."
"The boy, swimming in the ocean."
"She had lots of health problems. Like an irregular heartbeat and migraine headaches."

Fragments (dependent clauses) often occur because the writer is depending on the sentence previous to the fragment to complete the idea: "I know he didn't commit the crime. Because he was at the movies." However, in academic writing, you must not write in conversational fragments. Each word grouping must be a complete sentence. If a clause starts with a subordinating word like "because," it can not stand by itself and must be combined with an independent clause.

Correct fragments in the following ways:

1) Combine the dependent clause with the independent clause. "I know he didn't commit the crime because he was at the movies."

2) Remember that an –ing verb is not a verb unless it has one of the helping (or auxiliary) verbs with it. Correct the example by saying, "The boy <u>was</u> swimming in the ocean." Another option is to leave the –ing as a descriptive phrase, and add the completion of thought. 'The boy, swimming in the ocean, was calmly stroking the water when the shark attacked."

   TIP: Memorize the helping verbs: am, is, was, were, be, being, been, will, would, can, could, shall, should, may, might, must.

3) Pay close attention to the first word of the sentence. Transitional words often cause students to write a fragment. Again, this error is caused by relying on the previous sentence for the meaning instead of paying attention to each of the word groups. Correct it by combining it with a complete sentence: "She had lots of health problems like an irregular heartbeat and migraine headaches." Another option is to make the second word group stand on its own: "She had lots of health problems. Two of the most chronic problems were an irregular heartbeat and migraine headaches."

IV. Correct Sentences

Once you understand the rules for sentence boundaries and basic punctuation, you will have no trouble recognizing correct sentences.

- Remember that you must have a subject, a verb, and a sense of completeness in each sentence
- All phrases should be parallel in structure
- Modifying clauses should be placed next to the noun they describe
- Commas must be used with conjunctions when combining two independent clauses
- Semicolons should be used only between two independent phrases
- Semicolons may be used to connect two related sentences
- Semicolons may also be used with a conjunctive adverb to illustrate the connection between the two sentences
- Length does NOT determine whether a sentence is correct. Some writers, Faulkner, Fitzgerald, and Poe, to name just a few, wrote perfectly correct sentences of a hundred words or more. A one-word sentence, if it's a direct command, like, "Wait!" can also be a correct sentence. Don't fall into the trap of believing that just because it's a long sentence, it must be a run-on. Study the punctuation and the meaning, and determine whether the essential rules have been followed.

Sample Test Questions

Just for practice, look at the following groups of phrases and circle the letter of the correct sentence.

(Variations of sentences from F. Scott Fitzgerald's *The Great Gatsby*.)

1)
- A. The interior, unprosperous and bare; the only car visible was the dust-covered wreck of a Ford which crouched in a dim corner.
- B. The interior was unprosperous and bare, the only car visible was the dust-covered wreck of a Ford which crouched in a dim corner.
- C. The interior was unprosperous and bare; the only car visible was the dust-covered wreck of a Ford which crouched in a dim corner.

2)
- A. A damp streak of hair lay like a dash of blue paint across her cheek, and her hand was wet with glistening drops as I took it to help her from the car.
- B. A damp streak of hair lay like a dash of blue paint across her cheek, her hand was wet with glistening drops as I took it to help her from the car.
- C. A damp streak of hair lay like a dash of blue paint across her cheek and her hand was wet with glistening drops as I took it to help her from the car.

3)
- A. Daisy and Tom were sitting opposite each other at the kitchen table; with a plate of cold fried chicken between them and two bottles of ale.
- B. Daisy and Tom were sitting opposite each other at the kitchen table with a plate of cold fried chicken between them and two bottles of ale.
- C. Daisy and Tom were sitting opposite each other at the kitchen table with a plate of cold fried chicken between them; and two bottles of ale.

4)
   A. The evening had made me light-headed and happy, I think I walked into a deep sleep as I entered my front door.

   B. The evening had made me light-headed and happy I think I walked into a deep sleep as I entered my front door.

   C. The evening had made me light-headed and happy; I think I walked into a deep sleep as I entered my front door.

5)
   A. Daisy took her face in her hands, as if feeling its lovely shape, and her eyes moved gradually out into the velvet dusk.

   B. Daisy took her face in her hands, as if feeling its lovely shape; and her eyes moved gradually out into the velvet dusk.

   C. Daisy took her face in her hands, as if feeling its lovely shape and her eyes moved gradually out into the velvet dusk.

Correct answers for the five practice sets above: 1-C, 2-A, 3-B, 4-C, 5-A

V. Sentence Variety

When you were young and just learning to talk, you often said things in the simplest way possible. You might have a conversation at night with your parents that went something like this: "Today I went to school, and I had recess, and I played with my friends. Then I came home, and I had a snack. And I played kickball with Sandy. Then I took a bath and went to bed."

Can you imagine reading a novel that sounded like a first-grade conversation? That's how writing would sound if all your sentences were the same, or if they were all simple or compound sentences. Learning how to incorporate different styles and different lengths of sentences vastly improves the quality of writing.

A simple sentence is one independent clause: **The dog swam across the pond**.

A compound sentence joins two or more independent clauses with no dependent phrases by using a comma + a conjunction or a semicolon:

Lucy played pinball at the party, and Jake flirted with the girls.

A compound-complex sentence contains two or more independent clauses and at least one dependent clause:

While we were eating, the waitresses cleaned the kitchen, but the busboys relaxed outside.

Although it was frigid, the ocean was blue and inviting, and members of the Polar Bear club jumped in with enthusiasm.

TIP: Remember that word length has nothing to do with the correctness of a sentence. Good writers vary the length of their sentences, intermingling short, emphatic sentences with longer, more complex ones. You may want to count the number of words in each sentence on a page. If they are all approximately the same, you'll need to work on combining some sentences, shortening some, experimenting with different punctuation, and making sure that you raise the level of writing to college-level sophistication by creating variety.

VI. <u>Agreement</u>

If a teacher tells you that you have an agreement problem, he/she is NOT talking about a conflict. That instructor is using a common term to point out that two items are not "in sync" with each other.

1. Subject-Verb Agreement: If a teacher tells you that you have an agreement problem, then you'll need to look at the subject of your sentence and the verb of your sentence.

    a. Subjects and Verb Must Match in Number:

    It may seem strange, but even verbs are singular or plural, and in English, the singular verbs usually end in –s. The subject and the verb must BOTH be plural or BOTH be singular:

    Singular: **He swims** in the pool.
    Plural: **They swim** in the pool.

    The most common error is in not recognizing whether a subject is singular or plural. Many errors in College Composition occur because a student doesn't know that the following words (indefinite pronouns) always take a singular verb:

    Another / any / anybody / anyone / anything / each / either / everybody / everyone / everything / much / neither / nobody / no one / nothing / one / other / somebody / someone / something.

The "-body," "-one," and "-thing" words always take the singular even if they "sound" plural, like "everybody," or "everything."

Everybody knows that the world is round.

Everyone looks beautiful in the glow of candlelight.

Everything tastes delicious.

b. Compound subjects take plural verbs:

The **corn, peas, and carrots are** homegrown.

Cussing and swearing remain a problem in the public buildings of our nation.

c. If the word "each" or "every" occurs before a subject joined by the word "and," then the verb becomes singular:

Every man and woman on this earth **has** a mother.

d. If two subjects are joined by the word "or," or "nor," the verb agrees with the part closer to the verb.

Neither the cat nor the two dogs are properly groomed.

Neither the two dogs nor the cat is properly groomed.

2. Pronoun-Antecedent Agreement: This error occurs when the pronoun of the sentence doesn't match its antecedents. Pronouns can be either singular or plural.

The boys and girls fought to maintain their independence from their parents.

Every horse and mule runs at its own pace.

Every student in the room ran to pick up **his/her** bookbag.

TIP: Beware the use of the pronoun "their." One of the most common errors in College Composition is a problem with subject-pronoun agreement. For instance, a student might write, "A parent loves their child." The instructor would mark that as an error because "A parent" is one person. The pronoun "their" is a plural word, and therefore the two don't agree. The correct sentence would have both pronoun and its antecedent either singular in number:

A parent loves his/her children. (singular)

OR

Parents love their children. (plural)

If the his/her – he/she construction seems awkward and intrusive, then switch both subject and pronoun to the plural.

3. Pronoun Shift: Once you begin an essay or paper, be consistent with the pronouns you use. If you start out using the pronoun "one," then don't switch midway through the paper to the pronoun "he," or "you."

   If **one** wants to travel, then **he** should start saving money now.

   If **one** wants to travel, then **one** should start saving money now.

   OR

   If **he** wants to travel, then **he** should start saving money now.

   TIP: Some instructors don't allow the use of the informal "you" in college-level papers. Be sure you have a full understanding of the expectations of this particular professor before you turn in your paper.

4. Tense Shift: Present tense is something happening right NOW. Past tense is something that has happened before now, and future is something that WILL happen. Once you begin a sentence, keep the tenses consistent unless you intentionally mean to show a difference in time.

   Patricia **laughed and cried** until she **falls** asleep. WRONG!

   Patricia **laughed and cried** until she **fell** asleep. RIGHT!

VII. *Correct Idiom*

Foreign speakers often have trouble with idioms, phrases that are difficult to comprehend because they don't have a literal meaning. Phrases like, "it's a piece of cake," "he bought the farm," and "raining cats and dogs." If English is your second language, you might want to invest in a dictionary of idioms and colloquial sayings, and above all, listen to expressions used in daily conversation so that you can begin to understand the "figurative" language that is so often a part of life.

One idiomatic phrase that that's difficult to distinguish is the use of prepositions. "In" and "on" are particularly hard.

The word "in" is typically used when referring to something that occurs in a particular time or space:

The plane arrived in Florida after a storm delay.

The word "on" is typically used with dates and street names.

He was born on May 11, 1958.
He was lost on First Avenue.

VIII. *Active Voice*

The preferred kind of sentence in the English language, it simply means that the subject of the sentence is doing the action.

"The cat chased the mouse" is an active sentence. The cat is performing the action, "chased."

The same sentence becomes passive, however, if the subject is being acted upon instead of performing the action: "The mouse was chased by the cat."

For the vast majority of the time, sentences should be written in the active voice.

IX. *Logical Comparisons*

Whenever you compare two things, the analogy should be clear, logical, easy-to-understand and parallel in structure.

She had always expressed more interest in writing than dancing.
NOT PARALLEL

She had always expressed more interest in writing than she had in dancing.
CORRECT

The engine on the Ford truck was better than the Chevy.
UNCLEAR

The engine on the Ford truck was better than the engine on the Chevy truck.
CORRECT

His parents were wealthier than smart.
UNCLEAR / UNPARALLEL

His parents had more money than they had intelligence.
CORRECT

X. *Punctuation*

1. Commas

    Probably the cause of more errors than other punctuation, don't fear the common comma. All you need is some basic guidelines to whip this little device into shape.

    Forget any teacher who told you to put a comma in wherever you pause. That's bad advice! Commas are used for specific reasons:

    a. To hold together two independent clauses WITH a conjunction.
    b. To set off any introductory word, dependent phrase, or descriptive clause that comes at the beginning of a sentence.
    c. To separate non-essential information from the rest of the sentence.
    d. To separate items in a series.
    e. To set off transitional expressions or parenthetical information.
    f. To set off direct addresses, interjections, and tag questions.
    g. To set off quotations.
    h. To set off parts of addresses, titles, numbers, and dates.

2. Semicolons

    a. To link two closely-related independent clauses together.
    b. To link two closely-related independent clauses together with a conjunctive adverb.
    c. To separate items in a series containing other punctuation to clarify the meaning and make the sentence easier to read.

3. Question marks

    a. Put at the end of a sentence that asks a question.
    b. Use at the end of direct questions, not after indirect questions which often include the word "whether," or "that." (He asked whether I was going to the show. / She asked that I not tell anyone.)

4. Apostrophes
    a. Used in contractions to show where an omission occurs: can't = cannot / doesn't = does not.
    b. Used to show possession. An apostrophe + s, indicates that the item belongs to someone: The girl's purse was on the floor of the car.

       The bus's wheels were spinning in the mud.

       The men's fitness center was always crowded.
    c. Used by itself or with an –s to show possession of a singular word that ends in –s.

       Charles' favorite vehicle was an old Chevrolet Nova that he had rebuilt.

       Charles's favorite vehicle was an old Chevrolet Nova that he had rebuilt.

       (Either of the above is correct.)
    d. Used by itself to show possession of a plural word that ends in an –s.

       The three bridesmaids' dresses hung on the back of the door.

5. Quotation Marks
    a. Indicate direct, verbatim quotes.
    b. Single quotation marks are placed around a quote inside a quote.
    c. Placed around titles of short works of poems, essays, songs, articles, and individual episodes of television or radio programs.
    d. Put around definitions.

       TIP: Commas and periods are always placed inside quotation marks. Semicolons and colons are placed outside of quotation marks. Question marks and exclamation marks are placed inside quotes if they apply to the quotation itself; outside if the marks apply to the entire sentence.

6. Colons
    a. Introduce an example, appositive, or an explanation.
    b. Introduce a series, a quotation, or a list if the introductory material is a complete sentence:

       The wife made a list of all the necessary ingredients for bread pudding and directed her husband to pick them all up: bread, sugar, milk, raisins, and eggs.
    c. Separate ratios, salutations on formal letters, Biblical references, and elements of time.

7. Ellipsis
    a. Use an ellipsis to indicate where words have been omitted from a quoted passage.

Sample Test Questions

IDENTIFYING SENTENCE ERRORS

Directions: The following sentences test your knowledge of grammar, usage, diction (choice of words) and idiom.

Some sentences are correct.

No sentence contains more than one error.

You will find that the error, if there is one, is underlined and lettered. Assume that elements of the sentence that are not underlined are correct and cannot be changed. In choosing answers, follow the requirements of standard written English.

If there is an error, select the one underlined part that must be changed to make the sentence correct.

1. Often <u>the subject of poetry and song</u>, a full moon <u>has been blamed</u> for the howling
                A   B
of dogs, the thirst <u>of vampires</u>, the advent of lunacy, and <u>increasing births</u>. <u>No error</u>.
                  C   D   E

2. <u>Relaxing with a cold drink</u> and <u>lying</u> on the beach in my bikini, <u>the dog</u> startled me
               A   B   C
when he barked <u>loudly</u>. <u>No error</u>.
               D   E

3. <u>While the crowds at an airport</u> illustrate the diversity <u>of people</u>, they also <u>empha-</u>
               A   B   C
<u>sized</u> the <u>universality</u> of human nature. <u>No error</u>.
 D   E

4. A <u>subtle delight</u> builds in me <u>as I smear the soap</u> over the slick metal and <u>lather up</u>
             A   B   C
the car that takes me <u>anywhere and everywhere</u> I want to go. <u>No error</u>.
                             D   E

5. <u>When the frost</u> is on the pumpkin, one has to <u>don gloves</u>, or <u>he</u> will get <u>very cold</u>
     A   B   C   D
<u>fingers.</u> <u>No error</u>.
          E

6. Every person in the store <u>ran</u> to claim <u>their</u> free ice cream <u>when the bonus prize</u>
                                   A   B   C
was <u>announced</u> over the loudspeaker. <u>No error</u>.
        D   E

7. <u>When</u> the young immigrant woman <u>arrived</u> by jet <u>on the United States</u>, she went
   A   B   C
directly to <u>Washington, D.C.</u> <u>No error</u>.
               D   E

8. The pastry chef thought she <u>was losing her mind</u> because she <u>couldn't remember</u>
                                       A   B
if <u>the chocolate cake</u> and the strawberry pie <u>was in the oven</u>. <u>No error</u>.
     C   D   D   E

9. An old proverb <u>says</u> that if one <u>lives</u> in a glass house, <u>he</u> should <u>not</u> throw stones.
                  A   B   C   D
<u>No error</u>.
  E

10. The man was <u>better-looking</u> than her brother, <u>smarter than</u> her father, <u>as rich as</u>
                    A   B   C
her uncle, and nicer than <u>her grandmother</u>. <u>No error</u>.
                                 D   E

Answers: *1-D, 2-C, 3-C, 4-E, 5-C, 6-B, 7-C, 8-D, 9-C, 10-E*

IMPROVING SENTENCES

The following sentences test correctness and effectiveness of expression. In choosing answers, follow the requirements of standard written English: that is, pay attention to grammar, diction (choice of words), sentence construction, and punctuation.

In each of the following sentences, part of the sentence, or the entire sentence, is underlined. Beneath each sentence you will find five versions of the underlined part. Choice A repeats the original; the other four are different.

Choose the answer that best expresses the meaning of the original sentence. If you think the original is better than any of the alternatives, choose A; otherwise, choose one of the others. Your choice should produce the most effective sentence – one that is clear and precise, without awkwardness or ambiguity.

1) If a nation values anything more than freedom, it will lose its freedom; <u>and the irony of it is that if it is comfort or money that it values more, it will lose that too.</u>
 –W. Somerset Maugham

    A) and the irony of it is that if it is comfort or money that it values more, they will lose that too.
    B) and the irony of it is that whether it is comfort or whether it is money that it values most, it will lose that too.
    C) and the irony of it is that if it is comfort or money that it values more; it will lose that too.
    D) and the irony of it is that if it is comfort or money that it values more, it will lose those too.
    E) and the irony of it is that if it is comfort or money that it values more, it will lose that too.

2) Nothing in the world can take the place of persistence. <u>Talent will not, nothing is more common than unsuccessful men with talent. Genius will not, unrewarded genius is almost a proverb. Education will not, the world is full of educated derelicts</u>. Persistence and determination are omnipotent.

   A) Talent will not, nothing is more common than unsuccessful men with talent. Genius will not, unrewarded genius is almost a proverb. Education will not, the world is full of educated derelicts.
   B) Talent will not; nothing is more common than unsuccessful men with talent. Genius will not; unrewarded genius is almost a proverb. Education will not; the world is full of educated derelicts.
   C) Talent will never do it: nothing is more common than unsuccessful men with talent. Genius will not do it; unrewarded genius is almost a proverb. Education can't do it; the world is full of educated derelicts.
   D) Talent will not; nothing is more common than unsuccessful men with talent. Genius will not; unrewarded genius is almost a proverb. An education will not; the world is full of educated derelicts.
   E) Talent isn't; nothing is more common than unsuccessful men with talent. Genius won't; unrewarded genius is almost a proverb. An education doesn't; the world is full of educated derelicts.

3) <u>When I knew I was going to live this long, I'd have taken better care of myself</u>. – Mickey Mantle

   A) When I knew I was going to live this long; I'd have taken better care of myself.
   B) If I knew I was going to live this long; I'd have taken better care of myself.
   C) If I knew I was going to live this long, I'd have taken better care of myself.
   D) If I knew I was going to live this long, I will take better care of myself.
   E) Since I knew I was going to live this long, I took better care of myself.

Answers: *1-B, 2-B, 3-C*

 Part II: Ability to Recognize Logical Development

I. *Organization*

Have you ever had a teacher tell you that your meaning was unclear, that you "rambled," or that your paragraphs were unstructured? All of these problems result from a lack of organization.

Contrary to popular opinion, the order in which ideas fall out of your head and onto the paper isn't always the best order. Most ideas need to be presented clearly in a logical progression.

Understanding the basic structure of a paragraph is essential to organization.

Some teachers want you to present a formal outline for your paper. Others will suggest that you have a written plan, perhaps less formal than a traditional outline. Still other teachers allow you to use mapping, clustering, or other graphic techniques to organize your material. The important thing is that you plan ahead of time the order of the presentation of your paper.

Some common organizational patterns are listed below:

Chronological presentation: A time-sequenced order. Evidence is presented from the oldest to the most recent. You could also work backwards, starting with the most recent evidence and working toward the first item of interest.

Least important to most important: You might want to list your details and evidence beginning with the most minor, least important points first. Each point becomes stronger and stronger until the evidence with the most weight is presented. This enables you to leave your audience with a strong final opinion that can't be refuted.

Comparison/Contrast: A strategy where you're showing how topics are similar and/or different. Basically, there are two ways to utilize this technique. First, present all the information about one topic; then present all the information about the second topic. This technique is called the "block" approach.

The second organizational pattern for comparison/contrast papers is the "point-by-point" technique. With this method, you discuss one point of the first topic and show whether it is similar or dissimilar to the second topic. Each main characteristic of a topic is discussed in comparison to the second topic, so you are skipping back and forth between topic one and topic two. This pattern is a more sophisticated pattern and more interesting to read than the simple "block" style, and many college professors prefer this strategy.

Spatial order: Another possible way to organize material is to present it in spatial order. This works particularly well for descriptive papers. Start with the details that are farthest away in your field of vision and work toward the details that are closest to you. You might also try describing the things that are closest to you and working your way to a "wide-screen" description. Either way is fine. The main issue is that you figure out a way to present your details and that you are consistent with this presentation. If you're starting with a description of something far away, then don't jump around to something nearby.

II. *Evaluation of Evidence*

"Evidence" may be anything that helps support your point. Details, anecdotes, quotations, descriptions, statistics are all considered "evidence" if they help to make your case.

In academic writing, you must be sure to evaluate your evidence. Just because you heard it on the street or read it on the Internet, doesn't make it true. Be sure to evaluate evidence to determine its validity. Is the fact distorted by memory or time? Is there a credible source? Is the idea logical?

Once you get to the college level, you are not able to just write off the top of your head (unless you're taking Creative Writing!). In general, your papers will be based on reading other people's writing and then responding to it. You will need to base your opinions on textual evidence and logical theory.

III. *Awareness of Audience Tone and Purpose*

Do you talk differently to your grandmother than you do to your best friend? Do you include the same kind of details when talking to your mother that you do when talking to your significant other? Is your language always the same?

Of course not. That's why it's important to consider the audience of your paper. Consider how different a paper would be if you were writing it for a junior high school audience instead of a college classroom. Think of the differences in tone between writing for an audience of physicians at a doctor's conference and an audience of kindergarten teachers at an education conference.

Make sure you understand the assignment. Ask your teacher questions. Guarantee that you know why, how, and to whom you are writing. Your paper will be improved, and it will be easier to write.

IV. *Level of Detail*

Whenever possible, use SPECIFIC details instead of GENERIC ones. College composition students often write too little, putting forward the briefest possible descriptions instead of details which create a picture for the reader. Remember that the readers of your paper do NOT have the ideas or experience that you have and can't possibly know what you're thinking unless you tell them.

Consider the difference in these two passages which discuss the early morning surroundings on a country farm:

"The morning dew glistens like thousands of diamonds decorating each finger of grass. Trees bask their leaves in the remnant of starlight, and somewhere a hoot owl calls. Embryonic beginnings of a sunrise in barely visible shades of lavender can be discerned just above the horizon."

"It's morning and the dew is on the grass. Trees stand in the last of the starlight, and somewhere a hoot owl calls. You can barely see the sun as it comes up."

Of course, some assignments call for technical, concise sentences, but many more assignments benefit from the addition of specific details which utilize the senses of taste, touch, sight, sound, and smell.

V. *Consistency of Topic Focus*

"Consistency of topic" really just means that you have to stay "on target." From the time you present your "thesis" (which we'll discuss shortly), to the time you espouse your conclusion, you MUST show the reader how one paragraph is related to another. You need to tie together your thesis to each paragraph, and connect each paragraph to another. Some instructors call this "tying together," this obvious "connectedness" between points as "cohesion" or "cohesiveness."

Cohesiveness happens when you effectively utilize transitions between paragraphs or between sentences.

Typical transitions include the following words and phrases:
Again, also, anyway, as a result, as soon as, besides, certainly, even though, finally, for example, furthermore, granted that, however, in addition, in conclusion, in the mean-

time, indeed, instead, likewise, moreover, nevertheless, of course, on the other hand, otherwise, therefore, even though.

Another strategy to create consistency and cohesion is to use sequential words. For instance, if you are discussing the three main reasons that students cut classes, you might introduce your evidence with words like, "First and foremost," "Secondly," and "The third reason…."

TIP: Many college students seem to fear the written word, using as few words as possible in a paper. Don't be afraid to verbally explain your thought progression. Transitions can, after all, be more than just a word or a phrase. Good transitions can be entire sentences that explain to the reader where you're taking them. It's okay to say things like, "Even though that's a strong point, there's another more convincing piece of evidence to prove my argument." Sentences like this hold all your paragraphs together and make the argument easier to follow and more logical for the reader who doesn't already know what you think.

VI. Sentence Variety

The gist of good writing is that it is interesting to read. Interest is created through strong word choice, but interest is also dependent on variety. (Have you heard the saying "Variety is the spice of life"?) If all your sentences sounded the same, the reader would be bored to death. Work on using sentences of different lengths and varying styles. For a more in-depth explanation, see Section I of this guide.

VII. Paragraph Coherence

As discussed in the previous section on Consistency of Topic Focus, Section V, paragraphs need to be tied together throughout an essay, often repeating the main idea or thesis so that the reader can tell exactly how each paragraph relates to the overall message.

However, within each paragraph, you must have coherence as well. This means that the relationship between each sentence is clear, and that all the sentences in the paragraph are connected to the main idea or "topic sentence" of that paragraph.

One of the best ways to create coherence within paragraphs is to use transitions to show your train of thought from one sentence to the next. (See Section V.)

Another method of creating coherence within a paragraph is to repeat or reiterate key words throughout the paragraph. Concentrate on varying the words so that you don't repeat the same exact word over and over, but rather that you reiterate the "meaning" of the idea through different words:

In the following paragraph taken from an essay entitled "Computers Inspire Fear, Fascination," the author uses the key themes of "Native Americans" and "computers" in several ways throughout the paragraph, giving it coherence:

"Like the <u>Native Americans</u> watching invaders with fear and fascination, I observe the influx of <u>computers</u> into our society. Little did the Native Americans know that their world would be irrevocably changed and their very being would be endangered. Little do we know yet about how humanity will be affected by the mighty <u>computer</u>, and we're left to wonder if the cost of <u>technology</u> is the price of genuine communication."

Notice how the paragraph also gains coherence from the use of the analogy between the Native Americans and the European infiltration of land with the infusion of computers into modern society. Continued analogy is another way to hold ideas together.

VIII. Main Idea / Thesis Statements

All writing is done for a reason: to prove a point, to give information, to influence a decision. Whatever the main idea of the paper is, it should be clarified. Your writing will also be improved if you know exactly what you're trying to do. (You'd be surprised how many college students just begin to "write," without ever understanding what it is that they need to accomplish by writing.)

An excellent place to insert your thesis is at the end of the introductory paragraph. Notice in the paragraph below how easy it is for the reader to get involved with the topic through the introductory material and know what the writer hopes to accomplish:

"It all started when I read that mysterious, taunting, opening line: "Last night I dreamed again I went to Manderly." From the time years ago when I immersed myself in REBECCA'S English estate filled with writing desks, chintz, flowers, and silver serving trays, I developed a craving for the hot, soothing, golden-topaz elixir called tea."

As a reader, you can surely tell that this article is about TEA. Remember that thesis statements don't have to be boring. Granted, in some academic writing the thesis statement will be drier or more direct than in others, but you can retain flair and still make an obvious statement about the purpose of the article.

IX. Rhetorical Effects and Emphasis

Notice in Section VII, Paragraph Coherence is discussed, and one of the methods for creating unity with a paragraph is the use of analogy. (An analogy is a logical comparison between two things.)

An extended analogy is also a rhetorical effect, which means that the comparison you've made in the analogy is carried throughout the essay, not just in one paragraph.

Another rhetorical effect is that of "repetitive emphasis." Here, you repeat words, sentence structures, or phrases:

"Now, even though it makes me sad, I can understand why the prisoners weren't mourned. Maybe there wasn't anyone left who knew them. Maybe they had done too much damage to hope that someone would still care. Maybe their actions had obliterated the love of family bonds." Notice the repetition of the word "maybe," emphasizing the possible scenarios.

"Recently, I read an essay that asked whether or not Anne Frank would still believe in humanity's basic goodness. Would she have written the same words if she could have known about her own horrible death? Could she believe in an innate goodness existing, as she did, in the hell of Bergen-Belsen? Could her mind even comprehend goodness in the kind of evil that murdered millions of people? Would she still believe that people are good if she had witnessed the Oklahoma City Bombing? Would doubt about the inherent virtue of people surface if she had heard about a mother who purposely drowned her own innocent children and then willfully tried to place the blame on someone else?" Notice the repetition of questions and similar style to drive home the point that there is much about human nature that can't be explained by Anne's innocent viewpoint.

Other rhetorical effects include

- Placing the most important information of your sentence in the independent clause and not in a dependent phrase
- Listing the most important information as the final item of a series

X. *Use of Language*

Words! Words! Words! Your paper (and your grade) is built on the power of the written word. In a College Composition class you can't, after all, "talk" your papers out loud. To improve your writing, follow the listed strategies:

1. Your paper should always sound like you, not a textbook. In the world of writing, sounding like yourself, a real person, is called "voice." Utilizing your "voice" doesn't mean that you can't be the best you can be and use powerful prose. It simply means that you don't need to use a thesaurus on every other word.

2. Use descriptive words.

   Thoroughly consider the alternate word choices. For instance, consider the number of words that would more accurately portray the meaning of "said:" *Declared, demanded, uttered, muttered, whispered, shouted, retorted, replied, answered, croaked, theorized, responded, debated, pleaded, begged, laughed* – to name just a few.

3. In general, it's better to use one strong word than two weak ones:

   "*The baby wailed*" instead of "*The baby cried loudly.*"

   "*The man whooped*" instead of "*The man laughed suddenly.*"

4. Avoid clichés, the worn-out old sayings.

   Make new comparisons that are fresh and unique:

   Not "white as snow," but "white as an albino cotton ball."

5. Don't utilize "sexist" language. Many people object to the traditional male pronoun to indicate everyone. Words like "mailman," and "fireman" should be changed to "mail carrier" and "firefighter." In order to avoid sentences where you have to use a male pronoun, use the plural form:

   NOT: "A doctor must find an office before he can set up a practice."

   BUT: "Doctors must find office space before they can set up practice."

XI. <u>Evaluation of Author's Authority and Appeal</u>

In order for your writing to have "authority," or "credibility," you must present logical evidence. As mentioned in Part I of this guide, the writing you will do in College Composition is usually based on outside sources, and rarely on your own opinion.

To give your own writing authority, you need to show that you've done your research, citing experts, statistics, quotes, or anecdotes.

"Appeal" can mean two things:

1) An earnest or urgent request

   The local police station might appeal to the local high-school students in an effort to stop drinking and driving.

2) The power of attracting or of arousing interest

   The speaker appealed to the sense of fairness the listeners displayed and won their confidence.

To give your writing "appeal," you need to understand the audience, tone, and purpose of the assignment. If you know who you're talking to, and you know what you're trying to accomplish, and you understand WHY you're writing at all, you've mastered the art of "appeal."

But "appeal" isn't just an aspect of your own writing. It can also be used to evaluate outside sources. For instance, if you ascertain WHY an author is writing an article, you may more easily evaluate the validity of his claims. Beware of articles that are biased from the beginning. For instance, if a staunch supporter of gun use who is a member of the National Rifle Association is writing about the safety of guns, he will probably filter or not present information that suggests that guns are dangerous. Chances are, he'll appeal to your emotional sense of freedom and "the right to bear arms."

On the other hand, someone who has experienced great tragedy due to the use of illegal firearms will filter out or not present information that demonstrates safe use of guns and will appeal to your emotional sense of fear. Whatever the argument, pay attention to the authority and the appeal of the author in order to evaluate the validity of the article.

XII. *Evaluation of Reasoning*

Two main types of reasoning exist and are used to convince or persuade:

1. Inductive reasoning occurs when a generalization is made based on a number of specific instances.

    "I have ridden a roller coaster a dozen times in the last year, and every single time, I've gotten sick after the ride stopped."

    Inductive reasoning would say that based on a specific number of instances, the general statement could be made:

    "Riding roller coasters makes me sick."

2. Deductive reasoning occurs when a general principle is applied to a specific case.

    "Because riding roller coasters makes me sick, trips on 'the Teacup' will also make me sick." Deductive reasoning is much trickier than inductive because there are often no definitive answers. The reader must agree with the major statement in the first part of the deduction.

When evaluating the reasoning of an argument, make sure that each part of a statement is true, and that all claims are backed up by some kind of evidence.

XIII. <u>Shift in Point of View</u>

When you write, you may opt to use the *first person point-of-view*, I or we.

The *second person point-of-view* is using "you." (Before you utilize the word "you," addressing the reader on an informal basis, clarify with your instructor whether or not he/she allows that kind of informality.)

The *third person point-of-view* means using the pronouns, "he, she, it, or they."

Whatever point-of-view you choose, be consistent.

"The entire continuum of care exists under one roof. A leader in cancer education, the Cancer Center has served the area for more than a decade. The Center has a full staff of registered doctors and nurses to aid our patients. We have a special treatment room where you can watch television as your chemotherapy is being delivered. The staff is caring and compassionate, and they are all Board Certified. "

Notice the inconsistencies between the use of the point of view from "the Cancer Center" (it) to "we," and "they," as well as the switch from the word "patients" to "you." Pick a point-of-view and stick with it!

XIV. <u>5 X 5 Paragraph Essay</u>

A 5x5 paragraph essay is one of the most basic forms of essay writing. It breaks the essay down into five sections: the introduction, three body paragraphs and the conclusion. Each section should contain five sentences. For the introduction paragraph, the first line should be the thesis. The thesis is followed by three supporting statements, and the final line leads into the next paragraph. The three body paragraphs all follow the same format, with the first line taken from the supporting statements from the introduction paragraph (the first supporting statement starts paragraph two, the second starts paragraph three and the third starts paragraph four). Each body paragraph should then contain three supporting statements and a concluding line which links to the next paragraph. The concluding paragraph should start with a line summarizing the point of the essay, have three sentences restating the original supporting lines and then restate the thesis.

XV. <u>Sentence Variety</u>

When you were young and just learning to talk, you often said things in the simplest way possible. You might have a conversation at night with your parents that went something like this: "Today I went to school, and I had recess, and I played with my friends.

Then I came home, and I had a snack. And I played kickball with Sandy. Then I took a bath and went to bed."

Can you imagine reading a novel that sounded like a first-grade conversation? That's how writing would sound if all your sentences were the same, or if they were all simple or compound sentences. Learning how to incorporate different styles and different lengths of sentences vastly improves the quality of writing.

Incorporate various simple, compound, complex, and compound-complex sentences in writing to give variety and make the writing more interesting. It is also helpful to incorporate different writing strategies such as comparisons, parallel syntax, and others to improve writing quality.

Remember that word and sentence length had nothing to do with the correctness of a sentence. Good writers vary the length of their sentences, intermingling short, emphatic sentences with longer, more complex ones. You may want to count the number of words in each sentence on a page. If they are all approximately the same, you'll need to work on combining some sentences, shortening some, experimenting with different punctuation, and making sure that you raise the level of writing to a college-level sophistication by creating variety.

Comparisons

One of the most effective ways to describe or explain something is by using comparisons. When writing it is important that all comparisons are clear, logical, easy to understand, and parallel in structure. Some of the most basic types of comparisons are similes, metaphors, and analogies.

Analogy: A comparison between two things on a basis of their similarity.

Simile: A comparison using *like* or *as*.

Metaphor: A direct comparison, often using *is* to describe something.

That comparisons must be parallel in structure refers to the construction of the description. In order to clarify analogies, the same phrases should be used with each element.

UNPARALLEL: She had always expressed more interest in writing than dancing.
CORRECT: She had always expressed more interesting in writing than she had in dancing.

UNCLEAR: The engine on the Ford truck was better than the Chevy.
CORRECT: The engine on the Ford truck was better than the engine on the Chevy.

UNCLEAR and UNPARALLEL: His parents were wealthier than smart.
CORRECT: His parents had more money than they had intelligence.

There are a couple of phrases that you need to specifically look out for when making comparisons that are referred to as connectives. These are pairs of phrases that always go together:

- Not only / but also
- Both / and
- Either / or
- Neither / nor

If a comparison is long or contains more than one element continue repeating the phrase to ensure that it is parallel throughout the comparison.

WRONG: **Not only** is she going to California this summer, **but** to New York.
CORRECT: **Not only** is she going to California this summer, **but also** to New York.

WRONG: I prefer this grocery store because it is **both** near my house **or** well stocked.
CORRECT: I prefer this grocery store because it is **both** near my house **and** well stocked.

WRONG: **Either** she should get a job, she should get an internship, she should do a study abroad.
CORRECT: **Either** <u>she should</u> get a job **or** <u>she should</u> get an internship or she should do a study abroad.

WRONG: **Neither** the cat **or** the dog is allowed to eat at the table.
CORRECT: **Neither** the cat **nor** the dog is allowed to eat at the table.

 Sample Test Questions

Read the selection and then answer the questions that follow. Some questions are about particular sentences or parts of sentences and ask you to improve sentence structure and diction (word choice). In making these decisions, follow the conventions of standard written English. Other questions refer to the entire essay or parts of the essay and ask you to consider organization, development, and effectiveness of language in relation to purpose and audience.

(1) Prom time and hero worship are inevitably linked in my mind. (2) Being five years younger than my sister, Melanie, I was always in awe of her friends. (3) I know now that the magic of youth and the love of my sister colored her friends with the glow of heroism. (4) But to this day, one of those people still withstands the test of time. (5) Every spring, I think of Tommy Nolan, a hero whose image will never tarnish.

(6) I don't remember much of the courtship between Melanie and Tommy except his first impromptu visit to the Johnson household. (7) On a warm spring afternoon when he first dropped by after baseball practice, my sister was cooking dinner and waiting for my parents to return from work. (8) Never a very attentive cook and flustered by his visit, Melanie burnt the potatoes and steak. (9) Of course, my father picked that day to ask Tommy to stay for dinner. (10) He almost made my sister die of embarrassment.

(11) That afternoon, my parents, who were militarily strict when it came to dating and boys, developed an early affection for Tommy. (12) Who, after all, couldn't love a guy who munched black steak and said that his steak was "crunchy"?

(13) Melanie became the princess of my world when she bought her first prom dress, a white chiffon, high-waisted gown bordered with deep pink flowers. (14) In a little sister's devotion, I thought she was the most beautiful girl in the whole world.

(15) While Melanie was my princess, Tommy Nolan was my prince. (16) The high school guidance counselor let Tommy borrow his gold Cadillac to take my sister to the prom. (17) He came driving up in this freshly waxed and shining car and emerged with his arms loaded, hardly able to see him from behind a stack of white boxes, gallantly charging up the hill to the front door.

(18) He was one of the only beaus to win my mother's heart. I watched, amazed and thrilled, as he presented on of those boxes of a dozen long-stem roses to our mother. (19) Another box contained a dozen long-stem pink roses for Melanie. (20) In addition, there was a beautiful, fragrant bouquet topped with a white, silk butterfly.

(21) Melanie and Tommy departed for the ball, leaving a dewy-eyed mother, two charmed little sisters, and a house perfumed with the scent of roses and the stuff that dreams are made of.

(22) Years later, Melanie saw Tommy. (23) He was balding and heavy, but she said if you looked into his eyes, they were still the kind, gentle, green eyes of the teenager who had captured her heart.

(24) <u>Every spring, I think of my sister's old boyfriend and how much money he had to pay for those roses, how much thought and effort he put into making a good impression on my mom, how well-mannered, good-natured, and gentle-hearted he always seemed.</u>

(25) Prom time is still years away for my daughters, but Tommy Nolan left me with the permanent hope that somewhere out there are sensitive, hard-working teenage boys who still value the affection of mothers, cradle the hearts of girls, and retain the image of hero.

1) Which of the following is the best way to combine sentences 3 and 4?

   A) I know now that the magic of youth and the love of my sister colored her friends with the glow of heroism. And to this day, one of those people still withstands the test of time.
   B) I know now that the magic of youth and the love of my sister colored her friends with the glow of heroism, but to this day, one of those people still withstands the test of time.
   C) I know now that the magic of youth and the love of my sister colored her friends with the glow of heroism; in addition, to this day, one of those people still withstands the test of time.
   D) I know now that the magic of youth and the love of my sister colored her friends with the glow of heroism; but to this day, one of those people still withstands the test of time.
   E) I know now that the magic of youth and the love of my sister colored her friends with the glow of heroism, so to this day, one of those people still withstands the test of time.

2) Which of the following possibilities best adds descriptive language to sentence #8?

   A) Never a very attentive cook and flustered by his visit, Melanie burnt the potatoes and steak black.
   B) Never a very attentive cook and flustered by his visit, Melanie burnt the potatoes to a blackened film on the pan and the steak.
   C) Never a very attentive cook and flustered by his visit, Melanie burnt the potatoes to a blackened film on the pan and the steak was absolutely crunchy.
   D) Never a very attentive cook and flustered by his visit, Melanie burnt the potatoes to smelly black and burned steak.
   E) Never a very attentive cook and flustered by his visit, Melanie burnt the potatoes to a blackened film on the pan and broiled the steak to charcoal.

3) Which of the following possibilities best combines sentences #9 and #10?

   A) Of course, my father picked that day to ask Tommy to stay for dinner almost causing death-by-embarrassment for my sister.
   B) Of course, my father picked that day to ask Tommy to stay for dinner, he almost made my sister die of embarrassment.
   C) Of course, my father picked that day to ask Tommy to stay for dinner; since he almost made my sister die of embarrassment.
   D) Of course, my father picked that day to ask Tommy to stay for dinner, and my sister was embarrassed.
   E) Of course, my father picked that day to ask Tommy to stay for dinner; although my sister was dying from embarrassment.

4) Which of the following possibilities for sentence #12 most effectively depicts the incident?

   A) Who, after all, couldn't love a guy who munched black steak and said that he liked it crunchy.
   B) Who, after all, couldn't love a guy who munched black steak and said that he liked it this way.
   C) Who, after all, couldn't love a guy who munched black steak and said, "I like my meat a little crunchy?"
   D) Who, after all, couldn't love a guy who munched black steak and said that he ate it crunchy.
   E) Who, after all, couldn't love a guy who munched black steak and says that he likes it crunchy?

5) Which writing strategies do NOT appear in this selection?

   A) Comparison/Contrast
   B) Descriptive language
   C) Analogy
   D) Chronological Order
   E) Parallel Structure

6) Which word would best fit the beginning of sentence #15?

   A) Instead,
   B) Consequently,
   C) Moreover,
   D) If
   E) So

7) Which transitional phrase provides the best paragraph link for sentence #18?

   A) Unbelievably, he was one of the only beaus to win my mother's heart.
   B) Because my mother liked him, he was the only beau to win my mother's heart.
   C) On the other hand, he was one of the only beaus to win my mother's heart.
   D) No wonder he was one of the only beaus to win my mother's heart.
   E) However, he was one of the only beaus to win my mother's heart.

8) In the following sentence, which grammatical structure is being utilized?

   Every spring, I think of my sister's old boyfriend and how much money he had to pay for those roses, how much thought and effort he put into making a good impression on my mom, how well-mannered, good-natured, and gentle-hearted he always seemed.

   A) Irony
   B) Metaphor
   C) Analogy
   D) Parallelism
   E) Simile

Answers: 1-B, 2-E, 3-A, 4-C, 5-A, 6-D, 7-E, 8-D

Read the selection below and then answer the questions that follow:

(1) "The story of a woman who left her family in search of self-fulfillment wouldn't be given a second thought in today's world. (2) But almost a hundred years ago, society was shocked by the story of Edna Pontellier, the charming, intelligent, beautiful woman who left her successful, devoted husband and two children in search of some elusive happiness. (3) *The Awakening* by Kate Chopin, published in 1899, created a controversy by dealing with subjects thought to be "sacred." (4) As Larger Ziff says in his book, *The American 1890's,* Chopin's novel was censored because it "rejected the family as the automatic equivalent of feminine self-fulfillment." (5) The novel has been interpreted as an early feminist work, as a purely sexual "awakening" in the life of a woman, as the ultimate quest for self-fulfillment, and as the Naturalistic statement on life. (6) In truth, however, no single theme is dominant, for *The Awakening* integrates all of these elements into a central plot with the real message being that without self-sacrifice there is no true happiness and no true love."

1) In the third sentence the writer uses the word "sacred" to mean

   A) intensely spiritual
   B) exotic and mysterious
   C) religious, ritualized
   D) set apart from use; taboo
   E) frightening

2) Which of the following choices is NOT true about the phrase "As Larger Ziff says…." found in sentence #4?

   A) the author agrees with another writer
   B) the author disagrees with another writer
   C) the author is giving credit to another writer's ideas
   D) the author is using another writer's ideas to prove her point
   E) the author is paraphrasing another writer

3) The phrase, "rejected the family as the automatic equivalent of feminine self-fulfillment" could be more simply phrased as

   A) Family equals self
   B) Having no family automatically made a woman unhappy
   C) Family problems create selfish women
   D) Female self-fulfillment occurs automatically with a family
   E) Having a family does not automatically fulfill a woman

4) The main thesis of this selection is:

A) *The Awakening* is an early Feminist work
B) *The Awakening* is about sexual awakenings
C) *The Awakening* is about the quest for self-fulfillment
D) *The Awakening* is about Nature and its connection to life
E) *The Awakening* is about the effect of self-sacrifice on happiness and love

Answers: 1-D. 2-B, 3-E, 4-E

Read the selection below and then answer the questions that follow:

(1) By 1806 Napoleon had managed to conquer most of mainland Europe, he moved his attention to Britain. (2) The recent destruction of his navy meant that was not feasible for him to launch an actual attack, and instead he turned to an economic solution termed the Continental System.
(3) The purpose of the Continental System was to cut off Britain from foreign trade and aid. (4) As a mercantile country, Napoleon would then have the upper hand. (5) Another country would therefore be brought under French control without French forces having to fire a shot. (6) French guns were made by German manufacturers.
(7) The system was fairly effective in the sense that it did cause inflation and bankruptcies in Britain. (8) However, it also had negative impacts on French businesses. (9) Within a few years Napoleon was forced to allow trade with Britain to resume in an effort to raise gold which he desperately needed.

1) Where should the following line be inserted into the passage?

It ordered an embargo of all British goods by France and any countries under its control.

A) After line 2
B) Before line 7
C) After line 3
D) Before line 1
E) After line 8

The correct answer is C:) After line 3. Line 3 introduces the purpose of the Continental System, so following line 3 makes it the most logical place to clarify what it does.

2) This passage has which type of organization?

   A) Least important to most important
   B) Chronological
   C) Compare/contrast
   D) Spatial
   E) None of the above

The correct answer is B:) Chronological. The passage describes the effects of the Continental System over time. Therefore, the organization is chronological.

3) What revision must be made to sentence 4?

   A) As a mercantile country, Napoleon would then have the upper hand.
   B) This was ruinous for a mercantile country and Napoleon had the upper hand.
   C) France, a mercantile nation, would be devastated and Napoleon would have the upper hand.
   D) As a mercantile country Napoleon would, then have the upper hand.
   E) This would ruin Britain, a mercantile country, and give Napoleon the upper hand.

The correct answer is E:) This would ruin Britain, a mercantile country, and give Napoleon the upper hand. As written, line 4 contains a dangling modifier. This revision fixes this problem and clarifies the meaning of the line.

4) Which of the following additions to the end paragraph 3 would offer the most improvement?

   A) The Continental System was a low point of Napoleon's long-term war strategy, and in the end was more harmful than it was helpful.
   B) Other countries did not support the embargo, so Napoleon forced them into submission.
   C) Since this time, France and Britain have become strong allies and trading partners in terms of the world market.
   D) France had succeeded in subjugating many of the surrounding nations.
   E) An embargo is an order to cease trade, and in this case was an unsuccessful strategy.

The correct answer is A:) The Continental System was a low point of Napoleon's long-term war strategy, and in the end was more harmful than it was helpful. Paragraph 3 finishes describing the results of the Continental System. Option A is most appropriate because it summarizes the system and makes a nice conclusion to the passage.

5) Which sentence should be omitted?

   A) 1
   B) 3
   C) 5
   D) 6
   E) 8

The correct answer is D:) 6. The focus of the passage is the Continental System. Sentence 6 introduces irrelevant information.

6) Which of the following is the most grammatically correct way to combine lines 7 and 8 (reproduced below)?

(7) The system was fairly effective in the sense that it did cause inflation and bankruptcies in Britain. (8) However, it also had negative impacts on French businesses.

   A) The system was fairly effective in the sense that it did cause inflation and bankruptcies in Britain, however, it also had negative impacts on French businesses.
   B) The system was fairly effective in the sense that it did cause inflation and bankruptcy in Britain, it had negative impacts on French businesses.
   C) The system was fairly effective because it caused inflation and bankruptcies in Britain, and it had negative impacts on French businesses.
   D) The system was fairly effective because it caused inflation and bankruptcy in Britain: on the other hand, it too had negative impacts on French businesses.
   E) The system was fairly effective because it caused inflation and bankruptcies in Britain; however, it also harmed French businesses.

The correct answer is E:) The system was fairly effective because it caused inflation and bankruptcies in Britain; however, it harmed French businesses. Answers A and B are incorrect because a comma cannot join to lines without the additional presence of a conjunction. Answer C is incorrect because it incorrectly indicates that the system was successful because it hurt French businesses. Answer D is incorrect because the colon is used inappropriately.

7) What revision must be made to of sentence 2?

The recent destruction of his navy meant that was not feasible for him to launch an actual attack, and instead he turned to an economic solution termed the Continental System.

A) It should be moved to the third paragraph
B) "meant that" should be changed to "meant that it"
C) "economic" should be changed to "military"
D) The comma should be replaced with a colon
E) It should be split into three sentences to ensure that no run-ons occur

The correct answer is B:) "meant that" should be changed to "meant that it." Answer C is incorrect because it is an economic solution. Answer D is incorrect because the comma and coordinating conjunction "and" can be used to join the two independent clauses. Answer E is incorrect because the sentence is not a run-on.

 Part III: Ability to Use Resource Materials

I. <u>Evaluating Sources</u>

One of the most important parts of research is EVALUATING your sources. This means that you must read, comprehend, analyze, and sort out which articles are the most helpful to you and which ones are merely repetitive or lackluster.

Keep in mind the following guidelines:

a. Just because it's on the Internet doesn't make it true!

- Some college instructors do NOT allow the use of websites because, after all, anyone can build a website, and often, there is no way to verify the facts.
- Some college instructors allow you to use the websites of government agencies because they are dated and are often related to sources already in print.
- Some college instructors will allow you to use a website if you can document authorship, the date it was posted, and whether or not the organization has an existing bias toward the material.
- Finally, some college instructors allow you to use a website only if the information found on the website has a print analogue, which means that the material found there has been verified and printed in hard copy form.
- CHECK WITH YOUR INSTRUCTOR ON THE USE OF INTERNET SOURCES!

b. Even a piece of research that seems contrary to your stance may help you by giving statistics and data. It's also valuable to understand the opposing viewpoint to make your own argument stronger.

c. General encyclopedias may not be accepted as valid college-level sources, but you may be able to glean solid information from the bibliography included at the end of the piece. Since prominent authors and experts in the field are often hired to write encyclopedia articles, you might try searching under the name of the author of the entry to see if he/she has written any full-length works.

d. Be sure to evaluate any bias the article might present. For instance, a conservationist may write an article in a much different tone – and using much different information – than would a person working for a million-dollar refinery. This doesn't mean the information presented in either source isn't valid. It simply means that you need to be aware of the "slant," or purpose of the writer.

e. Books are often more thorough than articles, but they are also more often out-of-date. Consider your topic to determine whether books or magazine and journal articles, or a combination of both are most helpful to you.

TIP: Good research does not consist of pulling a stack of books off the library shelf and pulling tidbits out of each one. A competent researcher will use a variety of sources including the following: Books, indexes to specialized sources, journals and magazines, newspapers, documentary films, interviews, educational dissertations, speeches, and government documents.

II. *Integrating Research Material Into the Paper*

Research is different from other types of essays because it is not based purely on your opinion or your experiences, but in a large part, utilizes the statistics, theories, studies, and quotes of outside sources. In order to be able to write competent research papers, you must master the following skills:

a. Paraphrasing – restating, IN YOUR OWN WORDS AND IN YOUR OWN STYLE, exactly what the author said.

b. Summarizing – restating, IN YOUR OWN WORDS AND IN YOUR OWN STYLE, the main point or essential thoughts of the author's writing.

These skills are not as easy as they may seem. Remember that when you re-word research, you are not able just to use a thesaurus and insert a new word or two. The problem with this approach is that the STYLE of the writing is still not your own. It's also not enough to simply reword each sentence and leave the sentences of the original passage in the same order. Good research requires that the ideas be totally rephrased in your own style and vocabulary.

In order to accurately paraphrase an outside source, follow these guidelines:

a. Understand the "3 Word Rule": The 3-Word Rule is an unofficial guideline that means you should never repeat the same three words in the exact same order as the original author. If you follow this, you are forced to rearrange the structure of the entire sentence.

b. Understand that you need to read the entire passage and comprehend the author's meaning before you begin to paraphrase it. (Then, you are less likely to follow a sentence-by-sentence rewording.)

c. Retell the ideas in YOUR OWN WORDS!

d. Totally restructure sentences and the order of information.

e. Do MORE than change words with synonyms. (Even if you change a few words, you can still be charged with Plagiarism because you have not changed the structure of the author's original prose.)

f. Do NOT change the meaning of the original passage.

Ready to try? Take below the opening paragraph of The Declaration of Independence and put it into your own words using modern vocabulary, expressing your unique "voice," and maintaining all the ideas with the same meaning:

"When in the course of human events, it becomes necessary for one people to dissolve the political bonds which have connected them with another, and to assume among the powers of the earth, the separate and equal station to which the Laws of Nature and of Nature's God entitle them, a decent respect to the opinions of mankind requires that they should declare the causes which impel them to the separation."

Most research should be paraphrased or summarized. No one wants to read a paper that consists only of quotes strung together! In those rare instances where you do want to quote someone verbatim, you MUST include quotation marks around the words.

Any idea taken out of another source, whether it's a paraphrased statement, a summary of an article, or a direct quotation, must be cited.

As you work the facts and ideas from other sources into your paper, you'll need to give credit to the author and the source:

a. The first time you use any source, work the author's name, the title of the article or book, and/or some credentials about the author into the sentence. Giving the reader some ideas about the credibility of your references makes your facts more convincing.

b. You only have to fully introduce this information the FIRST time you use the source. After that, you can refer to it by the author's last name.

c. Be sure to introduce sources in more imaginative ways than by prefacing it with "according to…."

TIP: Much more interesting words to introduce a source than "according to…." *reports, suggests, points out, theorizes, advances the idea, supports, argues, questions, denounces, propounds, advocates, offers, proposes, advises, recommends, conjectures, concedes, hypothesizes, disputes, fights, counteracts….*

III. *Manuscript Format and Documentation*

When you "cite" a source, your instructor will tell you whether he wants MLA (Modern Language Association) form, APA (American Psychological Association) form, or another style. While the styles of documentation differ, the basics are the same.

1. A bibliography will be required.

    A bibliography is a list of all the sources you used to find your facts. Depending on the style of documentation, a bibliography will be called either "Works Cited" or "Reference" page. This page is the final page of your paper. Its purpose is to have complete publication information on each source so that if a reader found an interesting fact that she'd like to read more about in the body of the paper, she could turn to the bibliography to find exact publication information.

    Each source that you utilized will be listed with these three essential groupings of information:

    a. Author
    b. Title of work
    c. Publication data (dates, publisher, page numbers)

2. Each time you use a fact, idea, statistic, quote, or theory from an outside source, you must cite it in parentheses. "Citing it" means that you'll include vital information like the author, the date, and/or the page number from which you found that fact in parentheses immediately after the fact. (What you'll include in the parentheses depends on whether you're using MLA or APA or another format.) The information given in parenthesis is an abbreviation of the complete information listed on the bibliography page. The brief information in the parentheses enables the reader to cross-reference the source to the complete publication information at the end of the paper. This kind of documentation takes the place of the old-fashioned footnotes and is called "parenthetical citation" or "in-text citation.")

3. Some general rules about parenthetical citation:
   a. The author's last name is always the first part of a citation.
   b. If there is no listed author, the title of the article is used.
   c. No punctuation appears before the beginning of the parentheses.
   d. The only period for the sentence is placed AFTER the citation.

4. Some general rules about bibliographies:
   a. First part of any entry is the last name of the author.
   b. If no author is listed, use the title of the article or book.
   c. All entries are alphabetized by the author's last name or the first major word of the title.
   d. Bibliography pages have a heading in the top right corner, including a final page number.
   e. Forms are VERY specific with different punctuation and ordering applying to different types of sources. Be sure to check with your instructor about the appropriate form to use and then follow the guidelines for the selected style.

What about footnotes and end notes? What are they and how to they work? They are those little numbers you see while reading a book or a document like this[1]. Footnotes and endnotes basically do the same job. What is different about them is their placement. The information about a resource for footnotes are at the bottom or end of a page. Endnotes are at the end of a chapter, book or document. Both of these notation types are used to give the reader information about the source material of a certain section.

History is written by a process of argument. A good argument puts forward a point of view that is well grounded: it has evidence to support it. Unlike practitioners of other fields such as engineering or the natural sciences, historians pose questions that rarely have definitive answers or solutions. The emphasis in history is on an analysis of past events using a variety of historical evidence. Because much of the historian's task is interpretative, there are strict requirements regarding the correct citation of sources. Scholars use footnotes and/or endnotes for a variety of reasons including:

- To make it clear to the reader which views are yours and which are the views of other writers;
- To allow you to acknowledge your intellectual debts to others if you decide to accept their views or information;

- To direct the reader by the most efficient signposts to the place where the information you have provided can be checked and verified or where further useful information is.

Correspondingly, there are a number of situations where you MUST cite your sources.

- Direct quotations
- Any material that has been paraphrased from an outside source
- Any reference to arguments or facts (i.e. budget figures, technical specifications) that have been garnered from an outside source

There are also circumstances in which you SHOULD footnote

- To provide the reader with a guide to the sources used in the formation of the author's original argument.
- To provide the reader with a guide to sources that offer further information on ideas or arguments summarized in the author's text.
- To offer the reader further details or discussion beyond what could be reasonably included in the main text.
- If information is not common knowledge to the average lay reader.

Number of Notes

- If there is more than one sentence in a single paragraph that requires a footnote you may consolidate these by putting multiple sources in a single note and the end of the paragraph. If you choose to do this, you MUST arrange the sources in the footnote to correspond to the appropriate sentences in your text. You must also explain any potential ambiguities about which source refers to what information within the paragraph.
- You should NEVER use one footnote to refer to material in more than a single paragraph of text.
- So for each paragraph, you should ask yourself the following question: What primary and/or secondary sources did I use in the creation of this paragraph?

Web Citations

- While it is acceptable to cite electronic sources (emails, Web sites, online journals, online databases, etc.), if it is at all possible we would prefer to have the reference to the original material that was used in the creation of the electronic document.

- When referencing a Web site, it is imperative that the author include the date that the site was accessed online in the citation. In addition, the author needs to print out the electronic document for inclusion in the appropriate Historical Reference Collection. These precautionary steps ensure that if an ephemeral Web site disappears later, there will still be a record of the content material.
- Please do NOT cite on-line encyclopedias such as Wikipedia for several reasons. First, Wikiipedia does not list the author or creator of the information. Second, its content changes frequently. Third, encyclopedias usually contain factual information. (If you don't know certain facts, it's obviously fine to look them anywhere you choose, but facts typically do NOT need to be footnoted).

How to Cite a Newspaper vs. Book

Two commonly cited references are newspaper articles and books. The two have similar citations, but it is important that they are done correctly. For a book, the format is:

Author. *Title of Book*. City of Publication: Publisher, Year. Print.

The author should be listed last name, first name. If there are multiple authors only the first needs to be reversed. The title of the book should be taken from the title page (not the cover). The word print indicates that it was accessed as a printed source. The format for a newspaper is:

Author. "Title of Article." *Name of Newspaper* Date, edition: Page(s). Print.

Just as with a book the author's name should be reversed and separated by a comma, and the name of the newspaper is italicized. Notice that the name of the newspaper and the date are not separated by any punctuation.

IV. *Reference Skills*

Wouldn't it be nice if you typed the subject of your research paper into the computer and it gave you a list of sources that were perfectly suited to your topic?

It would be nice, but it wouldn't be realistic! Sources are catalogued in many different ways and with very different words. Here are some guidelines for making "research" go a little more smoothly:

1. Check the <u>Library of Congress Subject Heading Index</u>: This book will give you examples of the keywords used in categorizing your topic. Knowing how your topic is described by librarians and cataloguers saves you lots of time and increases the accuracy of your "hits."

2. Start up your engines! Search engines are tools which peruse the internet for information on your requested topic. Since all search engines are organized and indexed differently, it's a good idea to try more than one search engine to retrieve information on your topic. Some of the better known search engines are Google, Alta Vista, Excite, HotBot, InfoSeek, Lycos, and Yahoo.

3. Old-Fashioned But Worthy: While many indexes are online, you can also still go to the old fashioned print catalogues at your local library. <u>The Reader's Guide to Periodicals</u> indexes all the magazine articles that have appeared in the popular press for any given year. Learn how to use it because although many things are available in computer databases and retrievable through search engines, that information is often no more than a few years old. If you are doing historical research, or looking for perspectives on an incident that happened long ago, you will most likely have success in the print sources.

4. Specialized Indexes: Many magazines have specialized indexes which, again, are of great help in researching historical topics. Many of these indexes are indexed for the most recent years online. Check out the hard copy and the online versions of magazines like <u>National Geographic</u>, <u>American History Illustrated</u>, and <u>The Journal of American Medical Association</u>.

5. Indexes to <u>New York Times</u> and <u>Chicago Tribune</u>: Even though these are newspapers, they are NATIONAL newspapers covering all kinds of news, including historical topics.

6. Databases: Many libraries offer access to online databases. Check out services like InfoTrac, FirstSearch, Wilson's Select Plus, ERIC, and others. Articles and essays found in electronic databases are acceptable resources! Make sure you understand the difference between a database and a website. A database pools all kinds of previously published articles and essays from magazines and journals all over the world. This means that the information is more credible because you have a specific author, a specific publication, and a specific date. In other words, an article pulled out of a database has a "print analogue."

V. *Use of Reference Books*

When you do utilize reference books, you need to be able to understand the functions and the purposes of the books and their varying sections.

1. Encyclopedias: Most college-level instructors do not allow students to copy facts from encyclopedias. However, encyclopedias can aid researchers in supplying helpful bibliographies and the names of recognized authorities.

2. Textbooks and Reference Manuals: Used for substantive data and theory, textbooks and reference manuals are very thorough, but often out-of-date as soon as they are printed.

3. Glossaries: Often found at the back of textbooks, glossaries are specialized dictionaries that define the terms used in this particular field.
4. Indexes: Specialized publications focusing on one particular topic or field. For instance, there are indexes for medical topics, for business topics, for literary criticism, for film reviews. Such indexes give the precise publication data for articles that appeared on that topic.

VI. *Footnotes and Endnotes*

Footnotes and endnotes are used to give the bibliographic information of works cited in the body of a document. When using note style documentation, a number is written as a superscript after the information that is cited. If the paper uses footnotes, the numbers and the corresponding bibliographic entries for each page are listed four lines after the last line of text on the page. In endnote documentation, all of the notes are listed in a supplement to the paper. In both footnote and endnote notations, the citations are labeled chronologically according to how they appear in the text.

The form an endnote or footnote takes depends on the type of material being cited. Enough information should be included to allow the reader to find the source material if more information is needed. This table shows note documentation styles for some common types of material.

Examples of Footnotes

Description of Source Material	Example Citation Notes
Book written by one author	[1] Patricia Larkins Hicks, Opportunities in Speech-Language Pathology Careers (New York: McGraw Hill, 2007) 93. [2] Dorothy P. Dougherty, Teach Me How to Say It Right (Oakland: New Harbinger, 2005) 54.
Book written by two or more authors	[3] Froma P. Roth and Collen K. Worthington, Treatment Resource Manual for Speech-Language Pathology (Albany: Delmar, 2001) 201.
Edited book	[4] Lee Edward Travis, ed., Handbook of Speech Pathology (New York: Apple Century Crofts, 1957) 8.

Magazine Article	⁵ Craig Boerner, "Sleep Levels in Children with ASD," <u>Advance for Speech-Language Pathologists and Audiologists</u> 17.49 (2007):14.

In some academic disciplines, parenthetical documentation is preferred over footnotes and endnotes for citing sources. In parenthetical documentation styles, the source is identified in the body of the paper. For example:

> A hyphen is used to form compound words such as great-uncle (Stoughton 150).

The in-text documentation refers the reader to the appropriate entry in the paper's bibliography. The citation includes the author or editor's last name and the page number from which the information was taken.

If the paper drew information from more than one work by the same author, the citation should include a key word from the title of the appropriate source. Just enough information is required to help the reader identify the right source.

In the following example, the citation sends the reader to page 85 of <u>Harbrace College Handbook</u> edited by John Hodges. Just enough information is included in the citation to allow the reader to find the correct entry in the bibliography or list of works cited.

> The past participle form of the verb *to spit* is *spat* (Hodges, <u>Handbook</u> 85).

When parenthetical documentation is used, the complete bibliographic information for each work cited should be included at the end of the paper.

Footnotes and endnotes may also be used to provide supplemental information about the material discussed in the body of the document. Common uses for background notes in technical documents include:

- Explanations for missing or anomalous data in graphs, tables, or charts.
- Information tangential to the topic of the paper but of probable interest to the reader.
- Minor details about methodology that might influence a process's repeatability.

The example below shows how footnotes can be used to provide background information in a technical document.

Using Background Footnotes

> We decided to use the test field at Cooper's Ridge after the soil tests at the other sites showed high alkalinity.[1] We divided the test field into eight sections and divided different concentrations of the herbicide to each section. The number of visible *Viola papilionacea* clusters and the average number of leaves from a random sampling of clusters at each site was measured 1, 2, 3, 4, and 6 days after application.[2]
>
> [1] Although current research suggests the pH of the soil would have little or no influence on the herbicide's effectiveness, at the time it seemed important to test the compound on a soil with a chemical composition as close to that found at the Glen Oaks subdivision as possible.
> [2] Measurements were not taken on the fifth day after herbicide application because a rock slide on the highway blocked access to the test field.

Notes used to give background information should not be mixed with notes used for source citations. Background and bibliographic notes may be distinguished by using numerical superscripts for one type and alphabetical superscripts for the other. Alternatively, background notes may be used with parenthetical source documentation.

 **Sample Test Questions**

1) Which of the following would be the most effective way to introduce an outside source into your text the first time you use it?

   A) An article written by a psychologist from Harvard named Thomas Bently, claimed that the children who went West were more likely to succeed in the business affairs of the late 1800s.
   B) An article entitled "Children Who Paved the Way," claimed that the children who went West were more likely to succeed in the business affairs of the late 1800s.
   C) An article entitled "Children Who Paved the Way," written by a psychologist from Harvard named Thomas Bently, claimed that the children who went West were more likely to succeed in the business affairs of the late 1800s.
   D) An article entitled "Children Who Paved the Way," written by a psychologist from Harvard claimed that the children who went West were more likely to succeed in the business affairs of the late 1800s.
   E) An article written by Thomas Bently, claimed that the children who went West were more likely to succeed in the business affairs of the late 1800s.

2) Listed below are the first words of five different sources. Which would be the correct order to appear on the bibliography page?

   A) Payne, "Journey to the Moon," Boone, Tampas, Dalton.
   B) "Journey to the Moon," Boone, Dalton, Payne, Tampas.
   C) Boone, "Journey to the Moon," Dalton, Tampas, Payne.
   D) Boone, Dalton, Payne, Tampas, "Journey to the Moon."
   E) Boone, Dalton, "Journey to the Moon," Payne, Tampas.

3) What is NOT an advantage of using computer-based search engines?

   A) They quickly retrieve useful articles.
   B) They have significant numbers of historical archives from the previous century.
   C) They search multiple databases at once.
   D) They are accessible from home computers as well as computers in public facilities.
   E) They easily generate paper copy to work from.

4) The most important idea to be given in parenthetical citation is always

   A) The title of the source
   B) The date the source
   C) The author of the source
   D) The publication the source appeared in
   E) The page number the source appeared on

5) Which is the most accurate paraphrase of the following statement:

   "After Columbus and Cores had awakened the people of Western Europe to the possibilities, their appetite for converts, profits, and fame was thoroughly aroused and Western civilization was introduced, mainly by force, over nearly all the globe."
   - Introduction to The Columbia History of the World

   A) After Columbus and Cores had shown the people of Western Europe the possibilities, they wanted more converts, profits, and fame. Western civilization was introduced, mainly by force, over nearly all the globe.
   B) The population of Western Europe began to hunger for increased trade profits, enhanced status and more profit after Columbus and Cortes showed them it could be done. That is when Western civilization began to spread, and it spread almost all over the world, mainly as a result of conquest.
   C) When Columbus and Cortes awakened the people of Western Europe to the possibilities, the people wanted more converts, profits, and fame, which they got mainly by force, all over the globe.
   D) The people of were awakened by Columbus and Cortes, and began to see the potential for converts, profits, and fame, and Western civilization was introduced, mainly by force, over nearly all the globe.
   E) After Columbus and Cores had awakened the people of Western Europe to the possibilities, the people of this continent desired more converts, profits, and fame. Western civilization was introduced over nearly all the globe, mainly by force.

Answers: 1-C, 2-E, 3-B, 4-C, 5-B

Essay Writing

The best way to prepare for the essay writing portion of the CLEP examination is to practice writing. You will be writing the essay portion of the exam on a computer. This study guide will explain the structure you will need to follow when writing an essay. You will have 35 minutes to write two essays on a given subject. Only write an essay on the given topic in the exam. If you write an essay on a topic you create, it will not be accepted. At least five minutes will be spent thinking about the topic and how you will write about it. Practicing writing an essay within a 35 minute time schedule will reduce any anxiety you may otherwise experience at test time. There is no need for this anxiety. Try using the following essay tips for writing a practice essay. Choose a topic from the list in this study guide.

ESSAY EXAM WRITING TIPS:

An excellent essay will have:

- a clear thesis
- everything in the paper relate to the thesis
- clear organization
- appropriate connection between sentences and paragraphs
- a strong style
- command of grammar, punctuation, and mechanics
- no spelling errors

Be alert to the following instruction key words that you may come across in exam questions. If the question asks you to analyze something, it doesn't mean the same thing as defining it. These terms are not used interchangeably.

analyze	examine critically in order to bring out the essential elements of
apply	make use of as relevant or to apply a theory to a problem
assess	estimate, evaluate, or judge the value of
compare	examine two or more things in order to note similarities and differences
contrast	compare in order to show unlikeness or differences; to show the opposite qualities of
define	give the meaning of
demonstrate	explain or illustrate by example; establish by reasoning
describe	give a detailed account; list characteristics, qualities and parts
determine	decide upon; conclude or ascertain after reasoning or observation

discuss	consider and debate or argue the pros and cons of an issue. Compare and contrast.
distinguish	indicate or show a difference between
enumerate	list several ideas, aspects, events, things, qualities, reasons, etc.
explain	make clear the cause or reason of; to make known in detail
generalize	form a general opinion or conclusion from only a few facts or cases.
illustrate	give concrete examples; explain clearly by using comparisons or examples.
interpret	comment upon, give examples, describe relationships; describe, then evaluate.
justify	show or prove to be just, right, or reasonable
list	items written in a series that creates a meaningful grouping or sequence
outline	describe main ideas, characteristics, or events (different from a Roman numeral/letter outline.)
prove	support with facts
rank	make orderly arrangements of items
show	explain what is meant
summarize	write a brief and comprehensive recap of previously stated statements

Strategy for Writing the Entire Essay

Take a look at this online writing assistant site for essays http://www.powa.org/

1. Make sure your first paragraph contains your thesis statement. A thesis is a sentence that states the main point or idea of the essay. The thesis will give your essay direction. If the essay topic is controversial, the first paragraph is also where you will either agree with or disagree with the statement. In both cases, you will have to use supporting evidence. The side you choose has nothing to do with the score you receive. You will be scored on your ability to organize and write effectively.

2. Think of at least three supporting factors for your thesis and expand on those ideas with examples or illustrations. Each supporting factor should have its own paragraph. Use the scratch paper provided to write outlines or ideas.

    Useful transitions to illustrate an idea: For example, To illustrate, For instance, In this manner, In particular, Thus.

3. The last paragraph will be your conclusion. Your conclusion will be a summary of the points you have made on your thesis. Do not add a new idea in your conclusion. This is the time to give your essay positive closure with the last sentence. The reader, in this case the grader, should not feel abandoned in the last para-

graph. Don't give your essay that dreaded unfinished feeling. The thesis gives your paper direction, but it has to end smoothly too.

Useful transitions for your conclusion: In short, On the whole, To conclude, In brief , To sum up

4. It is easy to get off the subject of your thesis. Make sure you stay on track by reading your thesis after you write each paragraph.

5. The organizational style of your essay should be uncomplicated and straightforward.

6. If you have time, reread the paper when you are finished to look for:
    - Misspelled words
    - Omitted words
    - Incorrect grammar and punctuation
    - Incorrect dates and figures

Strategy for Writing Each Paragraph

TRIAC: Paragraph and Paper Organization

TRIAC is a writing strategy you can use for each paragraph to create a solid organization and an effective argument. TRIAC stands for:

T	Topic Sentence - The first sentence introduces the subject of a paragraph, and serves as a "minor" thesis statement.
R	Restatement or Restriction - The second sentence can restate or restrict what was written in the first sentence, making the subject more specific.
I	Illustration - This section of the paragraph consists of the illustrations (evidence, data, facts, quotes, etc.) that support your topic sentence. This section can contain several sentences.
A	Analysis - Explain, interpret, and contextualize the illustrations that have been made. Illustrations are not effective without the writer analyzing them.
C	Conclusion - The final sentence (or two) might review what the paragraph has discussed, and/or reemphasize what the illustration and analysis suggest. This closing section may also evaluate the connections you've made in your paragraph. You are setting yourself up to move smoothly and logically into the next paragraph.

Practice Essay Topics

Use some of the following topics to write essays or create your own essay topic.

(Try practicing writing an essay on a computer since the essay portion of the exam will also be on a computer.)

a) The images of children currently portrayed in the media are accurately depicted from today's youth. Agree or disagree.

b) Euthanizing animals in humane societies is actually not humane. Agree or disagree.

c) Explain what you think have been the main reasons for the increase in violent behavior in our schools.

d) Discuss changes that might occur if milk prices go up to $5.00 a gallon?

e) If you could influence the way products are advertised in the United States, what recommendations, if any, would you make? Discuss.

f) There should be a law restricting ownership of dangerous pets such as pit bulldogs. Agree or disagree.

g) The elderly are a precious resource that the United States is wasting. Agree or disagree.

h) Archaeologists have learned much about the lives of first-century Romans from the excavations of houses buried by lava at Pompeii. Suppose that your home were preserved just as it is now. What conclusions about modern life might future archaeologists draw from this evidence?

 Additional Practice Questions

I. *Punctuation*

CHOOSE THE LETTER IN FRONT OF THE BEST SENTENCE.

1)
   A) GM had started production of the cars in 1995 it was fully aware of the brake problems.
   B) GM had started production of the cars in 1995; it was fully aware of the brake problems.
   C) GM had started production of the cars in 1995, it was fully aware of the brake problems.
   D) GM had started production of the cars in 1995: it was fully aware of the brake problems.
   E) GM had started production of the cars in 1995, although it was fully aware of the brake problems.

2)
   A) GM recalled 48,000 cars in 1998 that recall did not solve the problem.
   B) GM recalled 48,000 cars in 1998 however that recall did not solve the problem.
   C) GM recalled 48,000 cars in 1998, that recall did not solve the problem.
   D) GM recalled 48,000 cars in 1998, although that recall did not solve the problem.
   E) GM recalled 48,000 cars in 1998, but that recall did not solve the problem.

3)
   A) Many people laughed at Kuhn, because he wore a suit and necktie to ballgames.
   B) Because he wore a suit and necktie to ballgames many people laughed at Kuhn.
   C) Because he wore a suit and necktie to ballgames, many people laughed at Kuhn.
   D) Because he wore a suit and necktie to ballgames; many people laughed at Kuhn.
   E) He wore a suit and necktie to ballgames as a result many people laughed at him.

4)
- A) Our class visited a water witch because we wanted to learn this art.
- B) Herman used forked sticks from Chinese elm trees, traditionally, willow sticks are used.
- C) Because water witching is a folk science; many people look on it with suspicion.
- D) He holds the stick by the forked end, and walks up and down on a piece of ground.
- E) He holds the stick by the forked end; and walks up and down on a piece of ground.

5)
- A) Dogs, that come in many sizes, are popular pets.
- B) Wolves, which were originally found all over Europe, are the ancestors of dogs.
- C) Wolves' tails turn downward; although dogs' tails turn upward.
- D) Dogs were domesticated all over the world, and were even owned by Indians.
- E) Wolves found all Europe, are the ancestors of dogs.

II. Combined Sentences

CHOOSE THE LETTER IN FRONT OF THE BEST SENTENCE.

1)
- A) Helen Murphy is crippled; therefore, she uses a wheel chair.
- B) Her wheelchair is electric-powered, it also has a fringed canopy.
- C) Because pedestrians complained to the police; she was taken to court.
- D) Although the pedestrians are safe through the week the Sunday morning joggers had better watch out.
- E) The pedestrians are safe through the week, although the Sunday morning joggers had better watch out.

2)
- A) Henry James wrote a story called *The Turn of the Screw* in fact the story has nothing to do with carpentry.
- B) Henry James wrote a story called *The Turn of the Screw;* however, the story has nothing to do with carpentry.
- C) Henry James wrote a story called *The Turn of the Screw* but the story has nothing to do with carpentry.
- D) Henry James wrote a story called *The Turn of the Screw* still the story has nothing to do with carpentry.
- E) Henry James wrote a story called *The Turn of the Screw*; although the story has nothing to do with carpentry.

3)
- A) Although the man employs her he never sees her again.
- B) Although the man employs her, he never sees her again.
- C) The man never sees her again, although he had employed her.
- D) The man never sees her again; although he had employed her.
- E) The man never sees her again however he had employed her.

4)
- A) Eighteen people have contracted the plague in New Mexico this year as a matter of fact there are more cases than in any state since 1925.
- B) Because there is a sever outbreak there this year several people have died of the plague.
- C) Several people have died of the plague in New Mexico, because there is a severe outbreak there this year.
- D) Until the cause of the plague is found people will continue to die.
- E) Eighteen people have contracted the plague in New Mexico this year; as a matter of fact, there are more cases than in any state since 1925.

5)
- A) Dragonflies have large eyes, that look like jewels.
- B) Dragonflies have large eyes which look like jewels.
- C) Dragonflies have large eyes that look like jewels.
- D) Dragonflies have large eyes; which look like jewels.
- E) Dragonflies have large eyes in fact they look like jewels.

III. *Possessives*

CHOOSE THE LETTER IN FRONT OF THE BEST SENTENCE.

1)
- A) The worlds highest mountain peaks have long been a challenge to mountain climbers.
- B) Most mountain peaks' in the United States can be climbed during a weekends vacation.
- C) Most mountain peaks in the United States can be climbed during a weekends vacation.
- D) The origin of mountain climbing seems to be tied to peoples' religious experiences.
- E) The Alps have always been European climbers' favorite area.

2)
- A) The ancient Greeks and Romans thought that their gods' home was on Mount Olympus.
- B) Mount Rainier and the Grand Teton are the United State's most popular mountains.
- C) The World Book Encyclopedias' sponsorship led to a famous climb by Hillary.
- D) Two of Hillarys' books are especially fascinating to those whose passion is mountain climbing.
- E) Two of Hillarys books are especially fascinating to those whose passion is mountain climbing.

3)
- A) Ichabod Cranes student's took revenge because he punished them.
- B) Brom Bones drawing of Ichabod made the teacher very angry.
- C) Brom's horses name was Gunpowder.
- D) Brom's horse's name was Gunpowder.
- E) Ichabod Cranes' students took revenge because he punished them.

4)
- A) Jody said that the drawing was her's.
- B) The Browns were proud of their new car.
- C) The three girls insisted that the money was their's.
- D) "Is it you'res," asked Mrs. Barberry.
- E) "Is it your's," asked Mrs. Barberry.

5)
- A) The dog was beautiful; I especially liked it's coat.
- B) The puppy's favorite activity was chasing its tail.
- C) After we started the tutoring program, some of our students test scores improved dramatically.
- D) Although I bought my daughter clothes in the latest style, she preferred last years' faded, ragged jeans.
- E) Although I bought my daughter clothes in the latest style, she preferred last years faded, ragged jean's.

IV. Subordination and Coordination

IN THE FOLLOWING SENTENCES, CHOOSE THE SENTENCE THAT DOES NOT HAVE A SUBORDINATION OR COORDINATION FAULT.

1)
- A) He is a person of great integrity, talent, and has the rare combination of drive and commitment that leads to success in the business world.
- B) He is a person of great integrity and talent and has the rare combination of drive and commitment that leads to success in the business world.
- C) He is a person of great integrity, talent, rare combination of drive and commitment that leads to success in the business world.
- D) He is a person of great integrity, talent, and is the rare combination of drive and commitment that leads to success in the business world.
- E) He is a person of great integrity, talent, but is the rare combination of drive and commitment that leads to success in the business world.

2)
- A) The players on the college team were skillful, prepared, but less committed than their counterparts on the high-school team.
- B) The players on the college team were skillful, prepared, and less committed than their counterparts on the high-school team.
- C) The players on the college team were more skillful, better prepared, less committed than their counterparts on the high-school team.
- D) The players on the college team were more skillful and better prepared; however, they were less committed than their counterparts on the high-school team.
- E) The players on the college team were skillful, prepared, less committed than their counterparts on the high-school team.

3)
- A) From the airplane, the river seemed languid, serene, and tranquilly flowed toward the sea.
- B) From the airplane, the river seemed languid, serene, and tranquil as it flowed toward the sea.
- C) From the airplane, the river seemed languid, serene, and tranquilly flowing toward the sea.
- D) From the airplane, the river seemed languid, serene and flowed tranquilly toward the sea.
- E) The river seemed languid, serene, tranquilly flowing toward the sea and could be seen from the airplane.

4)
   A) To hike the Appalachian Trail, one needs to be knowledgeable about survival as well as excellent physical condition.
   B) To hike the Appalachian Trail, one needs to be knowledgeable about survival, and should be in excellent physical condition.
   C) To hike the Appalachian Trail, one needs to be knowledgeable about survival and should be in excellent physical condition.
   D) To hike the Appalachian Trail, one needs to be knowledgeable about survival, be in excellent physical condition.
   E) To hike the Appalachian Trail, one needs to be knowledgeable about survival, and excellent physical condition.

5)
   A) Janie's professor told her that she should find a better place to study, she needed to spend less time visiting with her friends, and ought to attend class more frequently.
   B) Janie's professor told her that she should find a better place to study, she needed to spend less time visiting with her friends, and she ought to attend class more frequently.
   C) Janie's professor told her that she should find a better place to study, less time visiting with her friends, and ought to attend class more frequently.
   D) Janie's professor told her that she should find a better place to study, spend less time visiting with her friends, and she ought to attend class more frequently.
   E) Janie's professor told her that she should find a better place to study, spend less time visiting with her friends, and she might try to attend class more frequently.

V. *Identifying Sentence Errors*

IDENTIFY THE ERROR IN THE FOLLOWING SENTENCES.

Some are correct, and no sentence contains more than one error. The error, if there is one, is underlined and lettered. The elements in the sentence that are not underlined are correct. If there is no error, select answer E.

1) People <u>who hike</u> the Appalachian Trail <u>may stay</u> <u>overnight</u> in shelters if <u>you choose</u>. <u>No error</u>.
          A   B   C   D
       E

2) <u>College Professor #11</u> <u>teaches</u> <u>their children</u> <u>to write</u> biographies. <u>No error</u>.
        A   B   C   D   E

3) His son <u>grew up</u> <u>to become</u> a successful doctor, author, soccer <u>coach, and</u> have
              A   B   C
<u>a very successful</u> family life. <u>No error</u>.
        D   E

4) <u>My mother was</u> a very special woman <u>with extraordinary talents</u> <u>who made</u> a
          A   B   C
comfort able home <u>and was</u> a gracious host. <u>No error</u>.
                         D   E

5) <u>Convinced that</u> our community was not <u>well-informed</u> about the issues, <u>pamphlets</u>
       A   B   C
<u>were printed</u> <u>about the program</u>. <u>No error</u>.
     D   E

VI. *Improving Sentences*

In the following sentences, part of the sentence or all of the sentence is underlined. There are five versions of the underlined part. Choice A repeats the original; the other four are different. Choose the answer that best expresses the intended meaning. Choice A may be the correct one. Choose the one that makes the most effective sentence without awkwardness or ambiguity.

1) They associate <u>pain to being a hyper-consumer and pleasure to being frugal</u>.

   A) pain to being a hyper-consumer and pleasure to being frugal.
   B) pain with being a hyper-consumer and pleasure to being frugal.
   C) pain to being a hyper-consumer and pleasure with being frugal.
   D) pain with being a hyper-consumer and pleasure with being frugal.
   E) pain because being a hyper-consumer and pleasure to being frugal.

2) The reason I don't approve of research projects in schools <u>is because we must protect our liberties</u>.

   A) is because we must protect our liberties.
   B) ; however, we must protect our liberties.
   C) is that we must protect our liberties.
   D) is that, we must protect our liberties.
   E) is for we must protect our liberties.

3) <u>In this day and age the problem of smoking marijuana has had a much freer scope in recent years than was the case at an earlier period in time</u>.

   A) In this day and age the problem of smoking marijuana has had a much freer scope in recent years than was the case at an earlier period in time.
   B) Smoking marijuana is not as severely condemned as it once was.
   C) The problem of smoking marijuana has a much freer scope nowadays than it used to have.
   D) Today, the problem of smoking marijuana is more accepted than was the case at an earlier period of time.
   E) The problem of smoking marijuana is more accepted than was the case at an earlier period in time.

4) All the girls were looked on <u>as a sister in the camp</u>.

   A) As a sister in the camp.
   B) As sisters in the camp.
   C) Like a sister in the camp.
   D) Being a sister in the camp.
   E) To be a sister in the camp.

5) <u>Although there are many faults in the administration of the school, there are not enough to justify a change</u>.

   A) Although there are many faults in the administration of the school, there are not enough to justify a change.
   B) There are not enough faults to justify a change in the administration of the school, although there are many faults.
   C) Although there are many faults in the administration of the school, there are not enough to make it an unprofitable change.
   D) There are many faults in the administration of the school, therefore a change is justified.
   E) There are many faults in the administration of the school there are not enough to justify a change.

VII. *The Following is a Draft of a Student Composition with the Sentences Numbered for Reference*

Read the essay and then answer the questions that follow. You will be improving these sentences to solve problems in structure, usage, and diction.

(1) <u>The truth is most people are a combination of their met programs and internal and external frames.</u> (2) <u>However, if a child becomes too externally framed, they will be influenced by whatever the crowd is doing.</u> (3) The problem with this type of <u>thinking is the average person in the crowd is barely paying their bills</u> and certainly not a success. (4) <u>If Thomas Edison was an external thinker</u> do you think he would have discovered the light bulb? (5) <u>If John F. Kennedy was externally framed, do you think he would have ordered a military blockade against Cuba.</u> (6) <u>Or do you think he would have listened to Kruschev and allowed Soviet nuclear sites to be permanently established 90 miles away from Florida Keys.</u>

1) Which is the best way to rewrite sentence 1 to make it less awkward and to make its meaning clear?

   A) Most people are a combination of their inherited behaviors and internal and external frames.
   B) The truth is that most people are a combination of their met behaviors and internal and external frames.
   C) The truth is most people are a combination of their met behaviors and internal and external thoughts.
   D) Most people are a combination of their met programs and internal and external frames.
   E) The truth is most people are a combination of their inherited behaviors and internal and external frames.

2) Which is the best way to combine sentences 1 and 2?

   A) The truth is most people are a combination of their met programs and internal and external frames; however, if a child becomes too externally framed, they will be influenced by what the crowd is doing.
   B) The truth is most people are a combination of their met programs and internal and external frames and if a child becomes too externally framed, they will be influenced by what the crowd is doing.
   C) The truth is most people are a combination of their met programs and internal and external frames, in fact if a child becomes too externally framed, they will be influenced by what the crowd is doing.
   D) The truth is most people are a combination of their met programs and internal and external frames; although if a child becomes too externally framed, they will be influenced by what the crowd is doing.
   E) The truth is most people are a combination of their met programs and internal and external frames thus if a child becomes too externally framed they will be influenced by what the crowd is doing.

3) What is the best rewrite of sentence 2?

   A) However, if children become too externally framed, the crowd will influence what he/she is doing.
   B) However, if a child becomes too externally framed, he/she will be influenced by whatever the crowd is doing.
   C) However, if a child becomes too externally framed, the crowd will influence what they are doing.
   D) However, if children become too externally framed, he/she will be influenced by whatever the crowd is doing.
   E) However, if children become too externally framed, they will be influenced by whatever the crowd is doing.

4) What is the best rewrite of the underlined portion of sentence 3?

   A) Thinking is that average people are barely paying their bills
   B) Thinking is the average person in the crowd is barely paying his/her bills
   C) Thinking is the average person in the crowd are barely paying their bills
   D) Thinking is that the average person in the crowd is barely paying their bills
   E) Thinking is that average people in the crowd are barely paying his/her bills

5) What is the best rewrite of the underlined portion of sentence 4?

   A) If Thomas Edison was an external thinker
   B) If Thomas Edison were an external thinker
   C) If Thomas Edison had been an external thinker
   D) If Thomas Edison could be an external thinker
   E) If Thomas Edison might have been an external thinker

VIII. *The Following is a Paragraph from the Draft of a Student Composition with the Sentences Numbered for Reference*

READ THE ESSAY AND THEN ANSWER THE QUESTIONS THAT FOLLOW.

(1) Charles Henry is a successful general contractor who has built 47 communities in the southeast. (2) He remembers good times with his father building a clubhouse and a tree house in his back yard, where all the kids on the block used to play. (3) His father put him on the payroll when he was 11, and working on the weekends he earned enough money to pay for college. (4) However, after 3 years in college his father took ill, and he dropped out and helped him run the business. (5) He had so much enjoyment running the business he decided to earn his own general contractor license and is now Vice President of the company. (6) He says that even though many of his close friends are smarter and had better grades, most of them are struggling to find decent jobs.

1) Which of the following statements best describes the relationship of sentence 1 to the rest of the paragraph?

   A) It is the topic sentence; in other words, it establishes the organization of the paragraph as a whole.
   B) It is just the first sentence of several about the writer's background.
   C) It is not important to the paragraph as a whole.
   D) It could be left out without damaging the paragraph.
   E) It is an introductory sentence but not the topic sentence.

2) Which of the following statements best describes the relationship of sentence 6 to the rest of the paragraph?

   A) It is the topic sentence; in other words, it is the organizing idea of the paragraph.
   B) As the closing sentence, it completes the idea introduced in sentence 1.
   C) It is just another detail about the contractor's background.
   D) It is not essential to the meaning of the sentence.
   E) It is just extra information and doesn't play an important role in the paragraph.

3) Which of the following statements best describes the relationship of sentence 2 to the rest of the paragraph?

   A) It is the second part of a two-part topic sentence (sentences 1 and 2).
   B) It gives background detail that makes a bridge between the topic sentence (2) and the concluding sentence (6).
   C) It is just extra information and doesn't play an important role in the paragraph.
   D) Its purpose is to involve the reader emotionally.
   E) It begins a narrative sequence that leads from topic sentence to conclusion.

4) Which of the following statements best describes the relationship of sentences 3, 4, and 5 to the rest of the paragraph?

   A) They provide a narrative bridge between the topic sentence (1) and the concluding sentence (6).
   B) They merely provide background information.
   C) Together, they make up the topic sentence—the organizing idea of the paragraph.
   D) Their purpose is to involve the reader emotionally.
   E) They are interesting but not important to the meaning of the paragraph.

5) Which of the following statements best describes the relationship of sentence 5 to the rest of the paragraph?

   A) It is the conclusion.
   B) It introduces sentence 6, which is the conclusion.
   C) It restates the topic sentence.
   D) It is the topic sentence.
   E) It concludes the narrative sequence that leads to the conclusion.

IX. *Word Choice and Idiom*

IN THE FOLLOWING GROUPS OF SENTENCES, CHOOSE THE SENTENCE THAT HAS NO ERRORS IN WORD CHOICE.

1)
   A) Consuelo felt that Tonio's family did not except her.
   B) Tonio's mother made a special effort to show Consuelo that she was accepted.
   C) Tonio excepted a flying job in Buenos Aires.
   D) Consuelo sold all of her homes accept the apartment in Paris.
   E) The time in New York City was enjoyable for Consuelo accept the last few weeks.

2)
- A) Tonio was sure that the differences in their culture would not effect their relationship.
- B) Consuelo knew that if she married Tonio, her income would be affected.
- C) The affects of the invasion of France were devastation of the first magnitude.
- D) The downturn in Tonio's career was the affect of his marriage to Consuelo.
- E) The time in the south of France effected Consuelo's health.

3)
- A) Tonio's mother tried to make peace between all five of the children.
- B) The owner of the airline had to choose between all the pilots.
- C) The benefits were parceled out among the pilots.
- D) Consuelo and Tonio had to choose between the three homes in New York City.
- E) Tonio could not make a choice between the three offers.

4)
- A) The lawyer was chosen because he was an uninterested party.
- B) Vivian had become disinterested in marrying Tonio.
- C) Judge Jones must remain disinterested in this case if he is to make an unbiased decision.
- D) Her former ardor had turned to disinterest.
- E) Consuelo was disinterested in moving to New York City.

5)
- A) Eventually, Tonio and Consuelo emigrated from Paris.
- B) Many Puerto Rican natives have emigrated to New York City in the last 50 years.
- C) Most U.S. citizens are the offspring of ancestors who immigrated to this country.
- D) People are emigrating from Mexico in large numbers.
- E) There were many French emigrations to America following the German invasion.

X. *Verb Forms*

CHOOSE THE SENTENCE THAT DOES NOT HAVE AN ERROR IN VERB FORM.

1)
   A) The legs of the chair will be replace because they are wore.
   B) The dish had fell from the counter.
   C) I know that you have never drunk better orange juice.
   D) They believed that their son had died when the ship sunk.
   E) She announced that she was going to lay down and rest for awhile.

2)
   A) He had lead his country to victory.
   B) We have began using a new dry cleaner.
   C) The seam of the mattress had busted.
   D) He polished the furniture until it shined.
   E) The supervisor has spoken to the men about locking the door at night.

3)
   A) The books were lain on the table.
   B) We had shone her all the dresses in the store.
   C) My mother-in-law always complained that the dry cleaner had shrunk her clothes.
   D) I have not forgot the work I promised to do.
   E) This secretary had sat the folders down very carefully.

4)
   A) I had ran the same ad in the paper three times.
   B) Miss Clark has already shown us all the new products.
   C) The bedspread was already tore when I bought it.
   D) My granddaughter had
   E) He had showed me the steps in the process.

5)
   A) How many gallons of gas have we boughten this year?
   B) He has drove here from Phoenix three times.
   C) He has got three parking tickets.
   D) He laid down to rest after the grueling trip.
   E) He lay down to rest after the grueling trip.

Answer Key

I. PUNCTUATION
1. B
2. E
3. C
4. A
5. B

II. COMBINED SENTENCES
1. A
2. B
3. B
4. E
5. C

III. POSSESSIVES
1. E
2. A
3. D
4. B
5. B

IV. SUBORDINATION AND COORDINATION
1. B
2. D
3. B
4. C
5. B

V. IDENTIFYING SENTENCE ERRORS
1. D
2. C
3. D
4. E
5. C

VI. IMPROVING SENTENCES
1. D
2. A
3. D
4. B
5. A

VII. IMPROVING SENTENCES
1. A
2. A
3. E
4. A
5. C

VIII. PARAGRAPH STRUCTURE
1. A
2. B
3. E
4. A
5. E

IX. WORD CHOICE
1. B
2. B
3. C
4. C
5. A

X. VERB FORMS
1. C
2. E
3. C
4. B
5. E

 Additional Sample Test Questions

Composition

1) When Columbus <u>sailed</u> from Spain in 1492 he <u>was</u> actually looking for a passage
                   A   B
   to India. When he reached America he <u>assumed</u> he had been successful and
                                             C
   <u>had called</u> the native people Indians. <u>No error</u>.
       D   E

2) Mass <u>transit</u>, or public transportation, refers to transportation systems which <u>are</u>
           A   B
   available to the general public. <u>Including;</u> busses, trams, <u>subways and</u> other such
                                           C   D
   transportation systems. <u>No error</u>.
                                 D

3) Fossil <u>fuels account</u> for about 88% <u>of</u> energy consumption in the United States.
                 A   B
   Of <u>that</u>, around 40% is oil, 20% is natural <u>gas</u>, and 20% is coal. <u>No error</u>.
       C   D   E

4) Cultural pluralism refers to situations <u>where</u> smaller cultural groups <u>are able</u> to
                                               A   B
   retain their cultural practices and still be accepted by the community. <u>Simply put,</u>
                                                                                                            C
   cultural pluralism is when more than one culture <u>exists</u> peacefully in close
                                                                                 D
   proximity. <u>No error</u>.
                  E

5) The Krebs <u>cycle</u>, also called the citric acid cycle, is the process through <u>which</u> a
                A   B
   cell <u>converted</u> carbohydrates, <u>fats</u> and proteins into energy. <u>No error</u>.
           C   D   E

For questions 6-12 refer to the following essay:

(1) An oligopoly is a type of market which is characterized by the dominance of a few large companies. (2) Unlike a pure competition market, in which companies operate relatively independent of each other, the companies in an oligopoly are largely aware of one another's actions. (3) In addition to monitoring each other's actions they use strategy to determine their own moves and predict the moves of others.
(4) One type of game theory, and the most popular, is the Prisoner's Dilemma. (5) Imagine that two criminals are arrested for committing a crime. (6) They are split up and questioned separately. (7) If neither of them confess, it is likely that they will only go to jail for a somewhat short amount of time, maybe three years, due to lack of strong evidence. (8) They are both offered a deal. (9) If they confess they will get a shorter term of one year, while their partner goes to jail for a long time, ten years. (10) This makes the optimal strategy for both to confess, and only receive one year. (11) However not knowing what their partner will do or say under pressure leaves them with a tough decision.

6) Where would it make the most sense to add the following lines to the essay?

   Game theory is an important aspect of oligopolies. It focuses on the reactions of members of a group in different situations.

   A) After the last paragraph
   B) After the first paragraph
   C) After line 4
   D) At the very beginning
   E) It would not make sense to insert the lines in the essay

7) In context, which of the following is the best replacement for the word "strong" in sentence 7?

   A) Convincing
   B) Muscular
   C) Legitimate
   D) Powerful
   E) Defining

8) Which of the following is the best revision to line 10?

   A) This means it is smartest for them to only receive one year, and confess.
   B) This will make the optimal strategy to be for them each to confess, so that neither of them will go to jail for ten years, and they will each only receive one year.
   C) This means the optimal strategy is to only receive one year.
   D) This means that they both should confess, and only receive one year, because it is the optimal strategy.
   E) No change

9) Which of the following changes must be made to line 11?

   A) Insert a comma after "pressure"
   B) Eliminate the word "tough"
   C) Insert a comma after "However"
   D) Change "leaves" to "leafs"
   E) No change

10) In context, what is the best way to combine lines 5 and 6?

    A) Imagine that two criminals are arrested for committing a crime; they are split up and questioned separately.
    B) Imagine that two criminals are arrested for committing a crime, and they are split up and questioned separately.
    C) Imagine that two criminals are arrested for committing a crime but they are split up and questioned separately.
    D) Two criminals are split up and questioned separately after imagining that they are arrested for committing a crime.
    E) Imagine that two criminals, after they are split up and questioned separately, are arrested for committing a crime.

11) Where would it make the most sense to place a comma in line 3 (shown below)?

    In addition to monitoring each other's actions they use strategy to determine their own moves and predict the moves of others.

    A) After "addition"
    B) After "monitoring"
    C) After "own moves"
    D) After "actions"
    E) None of the above

12) Which of the following best describes the main idea of the essay?

   A) To discuss the difference between pure competition markets and oligopolies.
   B) To inform the reader of the existence of oligopolies in today's world.
   C) To convince the reader that the best strategy when confronted with a Prisoner's Dilemma situation is to confess immediately.
   D) To discuss what oligopolies are, and what game strategy is.
   E) None of the above

For questions 13-22 consider the following story:

   (1) It was six year old Tommy's first baseball game and he couldn't wait to wake up that morning. (2) He was out of bed at the crack of dawn and began finding himself something to eat for breakfast. (3) His team had spent a lot of time practising, over the past three week, and he was sure that they would win. (4) He went to the cereal cupboard and pulled out his favorite cereal. (5) Then he went to the fridge to get some milk. (6) It was then that he ran into a problem: he wasn't tall enough to reach the bowls. (7) He considered his quandary for a moment, then went around the counter and pulled over a stool. (8) He ate his breakfast, proudly.

   (9) His breakfast finished, Tommy returned to his room and began looking for his uniform. (10) He went through every drawer and pulled out every piece of clothing. (11) No uniform. (12) He searched under his bed, in his toy chest and in his closet. (13) Still, though, he could not find his uniform. (14) He ran down the hall and into the laundry room, dumping out every basket of clothing until it was found.

   (15) Tommy dressed quickly and gathered up his equipment. (16) Knowing that it would be time to leave soon, he started practicing his swing and imagined himself making a home run. (17) Then, his mother walked into his room. (18) "Yes," he thought excitedly, "it must be time to leave now." (19) But her words surprised him. (20) "What are you doing?" she exclaimed. (21) "It's two o'clock in the morning."

13) Which of the following would best replace the word "quandary" in line 7?

   A) Dilemma
   B) Breakfast
   C) Choices
   D) Position
   E) Surroundings

14) Which of the following is NOT a revision that should be made to line 3?

   A) Change "alot" to "a lot"
   B) Change "practising" to "practicing"
   C) Remove the commas
   D) Change "week" to "weeks"
   E) All of the above corrections should be made

15) Which of the following revisions to line 8 is correct?

   A) He ate his breakfast proudly.
   B) He, proudly, ate his breakfast.
   C) Proudly, he ate his breakfast.
   D) He ate his proudly breakfast.
   E) No change

16) In context, which line should be eliminated from the first paragraph?

   A) 2
   B) 3
   C) 4
   D) 7
   E) 8

17) What does "it" in line 14 refer to?

   A) His bat
   B) His baseball
   C) His uniform
   D) His shoes
   E) His jeans

18) What would be the best way to combine lines 10 and 11?

   A) He went through every drawer and pullout every piece of clothing, but he still couldn't find his uniform.
   B) He pulled every piece of clothing, opened every drawer, and couldn't find his uniform.
   C) He went through every drawer, pulled out every piece of clothing, and no uniform.
   D) There was still no uniform after he went through every draw and pulled out every piece of clothing.
   E) None of the above

19) Which of the following revisions should be made to line 18?

   A) Remove the comma after "Yes"
   B) Move the period at the end from after the quotation mark to before the quotation mark
   C) Remove the comma after "excitedly"
   D) Capitalize "he"
   E) No change

20) In context, sentence 11 serves to

   A) Break up the monotony of the story through its abruptness.
   B) Bring the paragraph to a close.
   C) Show Tommy's calm reaction to the situation.
   D) Emphasize Tommy's shock because it is short and abrupt.
   E) None of the above

21) Lines 18-21 are primarily used to

   A) Display a larger meaning.
   B) Create a comic ending.
   C) Make Tommy look like a fool.
   D) Show his mother's annoyance.
   E) None of the above

22) Which of the following best describes the story?

   A) An excerpt from a historical novel.
   B) A passage from a scientific journal.
   C) A children's story.
   D) An excerpt from a literary work.
   E) None of the above

For questions 23-28 consider the following paragraph:

(1) Ethan Frome is a novel by Edith Wharton. (2) The book tells the story of Ethan Frome who had been injured in a "smash up," some years previously. (3) A flashback shows the story of Frome falling in love with his wife's cousin Mattie (who reciprocates his affections) who has come to care for her when she falls ill. (4)When his wife Zeena discovers this she intends to have Mattie sent away. (5) Frome and Mattie form a suicide pact, but instead the two are just permanently injured. (6) The book ends with Zeena caring for Frome and Mattie.

23) Which of the following corrections should be made to line 1?

    A) Italicize "Ethan Frome"
    B) Underline "Edith Wharton"
    C) Change the word "novel" to "work of fiction"
    D) Add a comma after novel
    E) Move it to the end of the paragraph

24) Which of the following would be the best substitute for the word "reciprocates" in line 3?

    A) Rejects
    B) Responds to
    C) Gives back
    D) Returns
    E) None of the above

25) Who does the word "her" refer to in line 3?

    A) Ethan
    B) Edith
    C) Zeena
    D) Mattie
    E) None of the above

26) Which of the following is a suitable revision of line 3?

   A) A flashback shows the story of Frome falling in love with his wife's cousin Mattie, who reciprocates his affections, who has come to care for her when she falls ill.
   B) A flashback shows the story of Frome and his wife's cousin Mattie falling in love after Mattie comes to care for her when she fall ill.
   C) A flashback shows the story of Frome falling in love with his wife's cousin, Mattie, (who reciprocates his affections) who has come to care for her when she falls ill.
   D) A flashback shows the story of Frome's wife's cousin coming to care for his wife when she falls ill, and the two of them fall in love.
   E) Any of the above

27) Which of the following revisions must be made to line 2?

   A) Italicize "Ethan Frome"
   B) Remove the comma after "smash up"
   C) Change the word "previously" to "formerly"
   D) Change "had" to "has"
   E) No revisions needed

28) Which of the following best describes the main point of the paragraph?

   A) To describe the irony of the clichéd situation.
   B) To convince the reader that *Ethan Frome* is a literary work.
   C) To caution readers against forming suicide pacts.
   D) To summarize the events of the novel *Ethan Frome*.
   E) None of the above

For questions 28 - 32 consider the following paragraph:

(1) Strip cropping is a type of farming in which crops are planted in alternating strips, with one being the crop, and the other being some sort of grass or hay. (2) The strips are then lined at a right angle against wind, or slopes to maximize erosion prevention. (3) Contour cropping is a type of farming in which planting is along contours instead of up and down slopes. (4) This way excess water runs into crops farther down. (5) The two methods are most useful when practiced together in strip contour cropping. (6) This is when the crops are planted in alternating strips which run along the contour instead of up and down a slope. (7) This helps to decrease soil erosion and makes more effective use of rainfall.

29) Which of the following would best improve the quality of the paragraph as a whole?

   A) A stronger conclusion
   B) More information comparing the two types of farming
   C) An introduction to the paragraph
   D) More specific examples
   E) Checking to make sure all words are spelled correctly

30) Which of the following would be the best correction to make in line 3?

   A) Insert "specific" before the word "type"
   B) Insert "done" after the word "is"
   C) Insert a comma after "farming"
   D) Change "up and down" to "on"
   E) Move the line to be after line 4

31) In context, line 7 serves to

   A) Better explain why contour cropping is useful.
   B) Tie up the paragraph and explain the benefits of strip contour cropping.
   C) Introduce the next topic.
   D) Offer a refutation of the preceding argument.
   E) None of the above

32) Which correction must be made to line 2?

   A) Change the word "maximize" to "minimize"
   B) Add a second comma after "slopes"
   C) Further explain what a right angle is
   D) Remove the comma after "wind"
   E) Move the line to the beginning of the paragraph

33) Which of the following describes the logic behind the organization of the paragraph?

   A) The methods are organized in order of how often they are used so that as the paragraph progresses the reader is more convinced to use the last method.
   B) The paragraph is organized in alphabetical order to make the paragraph seem like it has academic merit.
   C) The paragraph is ordered so that the first method is the least practical, the second method is the most practical and the third method is moderately practical.
   D) Strip and contour cropping are discussed first to give background information to help the reader understand strip contour cropping.
   E) There is no particular order to the paragraph.

For questions 33 – 45 refer to the following essay:

(1) The Civil War was one of the worst wars the United States has been involved in. (2) Although it was not necessarily the beginning of the war, the first battle was Fort Sumter. (3) What made it the Civil War so terrible was that every soldier killed was an American, meaning that the overall American deaths were greater than in many other wars combined. (4) The war started in 1861, but the tensions and problems that caused it were building for long before that.

(5) Slavery was one of the main issues behind the war; but it was not the direct cause. (6) What caused the first wave of states to secede was because of the election of Abraham Lincoln. (7) Not a single southern state had voted for him, yet he was to be the next president. (8) The war is considered to have begun with the secession of South Carolina, which was soon followed by the secession of Mississippi, Florida, Alabama, Georgia, Louisiana and Texas. (9) These states were later joined by others totaling 11 seceded states which called themselves the Confederate States of America.

(10) Fort Sumter was a military fort in South Carolina which the Confederacy demanded surrender. (11) Lincoln refused to surrender the fort and the Confederacy proceeded to bombard it. (12) Because relief did not arrive in time, they were forced to surrender and Lincoln began raising troops to take it again. (13) He got around the law requiring him to ask Congress for a declaration of war because he refused to acknowledge the Confederacy as a sovereign state, and instead viewed their secession as an insurrection. (14) So, the war began.

(15) The four year struggle between the two sections of the country changed the face the country. (16) Extensive damage had been done to areas where fighting occurred and even a new state was created (West Virginia). (17) However the war had positive aspects as well. (18) It kept the country together, and showed the states that the Federal government would not allow them disregard laws. (19) It also provided a way for the abolition of slavery.

34) Which of the following corrections should be made to line 3?

    A) Move it to the end of the essay
    B) Add a comma after the word "it"
    C) Put a question mark at the end instead of a period because it starts with an interrogative pronoun
    D) Remove the word "it"
    E) None of the above

35) Which of the following line changes should be made to improve the flow of the essay?

   A) Move line 2 to be after line 9
   B) Move line 6 to be before line 5
   C) Move line 8 to be after line 6
   D) Move line 11 to after line 13
   E) Move line 15 the beginning of the essay

36) Which of the following corrections should be made to line 5?

   A) Change the semicolon to a colon
   B) Change the semicolon to a comma
   C) Add a comma after "but"
   D) Change "issues" to "issue"
   E) Remove the word "direct"

37) Which of the following would most contribute to the content of the essay as a whole?

   A) Talking less about how the war was started.
   B) Checking for correct spelling and punctuation usage throughout.
   C) Adding additional information about the major battles and the course of the war.
   D) Do not refer to the southern states as the Confederacy.
   E) No changes must be made.

38) Which of the following corrections should be made to line 8?

   A) A semicolon should be added after "by" because it is the beginning of a list.
   B) A comma should be added after "Louisiana" because it is followed by "and."
   C) Only the name of the first state in the list needs to be capitalized.
   D) There should not be a comma following South Carolina because it is not followed by a conjunction.
   E) No changes must be made.

39) Which of the following is the best revision of line 13?

   A) Because he viewed the Confederate States as insurrectionary, and not as sovereign states, Lincoln did not need to ask Congress for a declaration of war.
   B) Lincoln was allowed to ignore any laws requiring him to go to Congress to ask for a formal declaration of war because he refused to acknowledge the fact that the Confederacy was a sovereign state. Instead he viewed their secession as an insurrection, which made it his responsibility to act.
   C) Lincoln acted without asking for a declaration of war from Congress.
   D) Lincoln was lucky that there was no law requiring him to get a formal declaration of war because most of the people did not agree that the south had no right to secede.
   E) None of the revisions is better than the original text.

40) Who does "they" refer to in line 13?

   A) The Confederacy
   B) Lincoln
   C) The relief
   D) Fort Sumter
   E) None of the above

41) What change should be made to the underlined portion of line 16 (shown below)?

   Extensive damage was done to areas where fighting occurred and even a new state was created (West Virginia).

   A) Move "even" to after "was"
   B) Add a comma after "created"
   C) Remove the parentheses around "West Virginia"
   D) Add a comma after "occurred"
   E) No change should be made

42) Which of the following would be the best correction to line 6?

   A) Change "to secede" to "secession"
   B) Remove "because of"
   C) Add "recent" before "election"
   D) Remove "What caused"
   E) Remove "first wave of"

43) Which of the following revisions should be made to line 17?

   A) Change "However" to "But,"
   B) Remove the word "aspects"
   C) Capitalize "war"
   D) Add a comma after "However"
   E) None of the above

44) According to the passage

   A) The Civil War was directly caused by slavery.
   B) The Civil War was inexpensive.
   C) One of the main issues of the Civil War was slavery.
   D) There was no legitimate reason for the Civil War.
   E) None of the above

45) Which of the following most correctly describes the main idea of the essay?

   A) To discuss the major battles of the Civil War.
   B) To explain why slavery was not the only cause of the Civil War.
   C) To describe the events of Fort Sumter.
   D) To convince the reader that it was noble of Lincoln to abolish slavery.
   E) To discuss effects and causes of the Civil War.

45) Line 5 serves what purpose in the essay?

   A) To provide a resolution to the problem introduced in the first paragraph.
   B) To describe the main reason for the end of the Civil War.
   C) To indicate that although slavery was an underlying factor in the war, there were other factors which led to the immediate start of the war.
   D) To indicate that slavery was not an important focus of the war.
   E) None of the above

47) How is the title of the article indicated when citing a newspaper article?

   A) Italicized
   B) Underlined
   C) Quotation marks
   D) Bolded
   E) Parentheses

48) Which of the following is NOT included in the citation for a newspaper article?

   A) Author
   B) Pages
   C) Head of newspaper
   D) Name of newspaper
   E) Edition

49) Which of the following is NOT included in the citation for a book?

   A) Author
   B) Title of the book
   C) City of publication
   D) Day, month and year of publication
   E) Publisher

50) In MLA format, how should the title of the book be indicated?

   A) Underlined
   B) Bolded
   C) Quotation marks
   D) Circled
   E) Italicized

Answer Key

1) D
2) C
3) D
4) E
5) D
6) B
7) A
8) E
9) C
10) B
11) D
12) D
13) A
14) E
15) A
16) B
17) C
18) A
19) B
20) D
21) B
22) C
23) A
24) D
25) C
26) E
27) A
28) D
29) C
30) B
31) B
32) D
33) D
34) D
35) A
36) B
37) C
38) E
39) A
40) D
41) A
42) B
43) D
44) C
45) E
46) C
47) C
48) C
49) D
50) E

Test Taking Strategies

Here are some test-taking strategies that are specific to this test and to other CLEP tests in general:
- Keep your eyes on the time. Pay attention to how much time you have left.
- Read the entire question and read all the answers. Many questions are not as hard to answer as they may seem. Sometimes, a difficult sounding question really only is asking you how to read an accompanying chart. Chart and graph questions are on most CLEP tests and should be an easy free point.
- If you don't know the answer immediately, the new computer-based testing lets you mark questions and come back to them later if you have time.
- Read the wording carefully. Some words can give you hints to the right answer. There are no exceptions to an answer when there are words in the question such as always, all or none. If one of the answer choices includes most or some of the right answers, but not all, then that is not the correct answer. Here is an example:

    The primary colors include all of the following:

    A) Red, Yellow, Blue, Green
    B) Red, Green, Yellow
    C) Red, Orange, Yellow
    D) Red, Yellow, Blue
    E) None of the above

    Although item A includes all the right answers, it also includes an incorrect answer, making it incorrect. If you didn't read it carefully, were in a hurry, or didn't know the material well, you might fall for this.
- Make a guess on a question that you do not know the answer to. There is no penalty for an incorrect answer. Eliminate the answer choices that you know are incorrect. For example, this will let your guess be a 1 in 3 chance instead.

What Your Score Means

Based on your score, you may, or may not, qualify for credit at your specific institution. At University of Phoenix, a score of 50 is passing for full credit. At Utah Valley University, the score is unpublished, the school will accept credit on a case-by-case basis. Another school, Brigham Young University (BYU) does not accept CLEP credit. To find out what score you need for credit, you need to get that information from your school's website or academic advisor.

You can score between 20 and 80 on any CLEP test. Some exams include percentile ranks. Each correct answer is worth one point. You lose no points for unanswered or incorrect questions.

Test Preparation

How much you need to study depends on your knowledge of a subject area. If you are interested in literature, took it in school, or enjoy reading then your studying and preparation for the literature or humanities test will not need to be as intensive as someone who is new to literature.

This book is much different than the regular CLEP study guides. This book actually teaches you the information that you need to know to pass the test. If you are particularly interested in an area, or you want more information, do a quick search online. We've tried not to include too much depth in areas that are not as essential on the test. Everything in this book will be on the test. It is important to understand all major theories and concepts listed in the table of contents. It is also very important to know any bolded words. Don't worry if you do not understand or know a lot about the area. With minimal study, you can complete and pass the test.

Legal Note

All rights reserved. This Study Guide, Book and Flashcards are protected under US Copyright Law. No part of this book or study guide or flashcards may be reproduced, distributed or stored in a retrieval system, or transmitted in any form or by any means, electronic, mechanical, photocopying, recording, or otherwise, without the prior written permission of the publisher Breely Crush Publishing, LLC. This manual is not supported by or affiliated with the College Board, creators of the CLEP test. CLEP is a registered trademark of the College Entrance Examination Board, which does not endorse this book.

FLASHCARDS

This section contains flashcards for you to use to further your understanding of the material and test yourself on important concepts, names or dates. Read the term or question then flip the page over to check the answer on the back. Keep in mind that this information may not be covered in the text of the study guide. Take your time to study the flashcards, you will need to know and understand these concepts to pass the test.

Syntax	Coordination
Subordination	Modifier
Comma Splice	Run-on Sentence
Sentence Fragment	Simple Sentence

How you connect ideas together	How words are put together
A descriptive phrase or word	How you make one idea subordinate to another idea
Two sentences put together without appropriate punctuation	When two complete sentences are tied together with a comma
One independent clause	An incomplete sentence

Compound Sentence	Compound Complex Sentence
Subject-Verb Agreement	Pronoun-Antecedent Agreement
Antecedents	Idiom
,	;

Two or more independent clauses with a dependent clause	Two or more independent clauses with out a dependent clause
When the pronoun doesn't match its antecedents	When the subject and verb of a sentence don't go together
A phrase without a literal meaning	Going before, preceding
Semi-colon	Comma

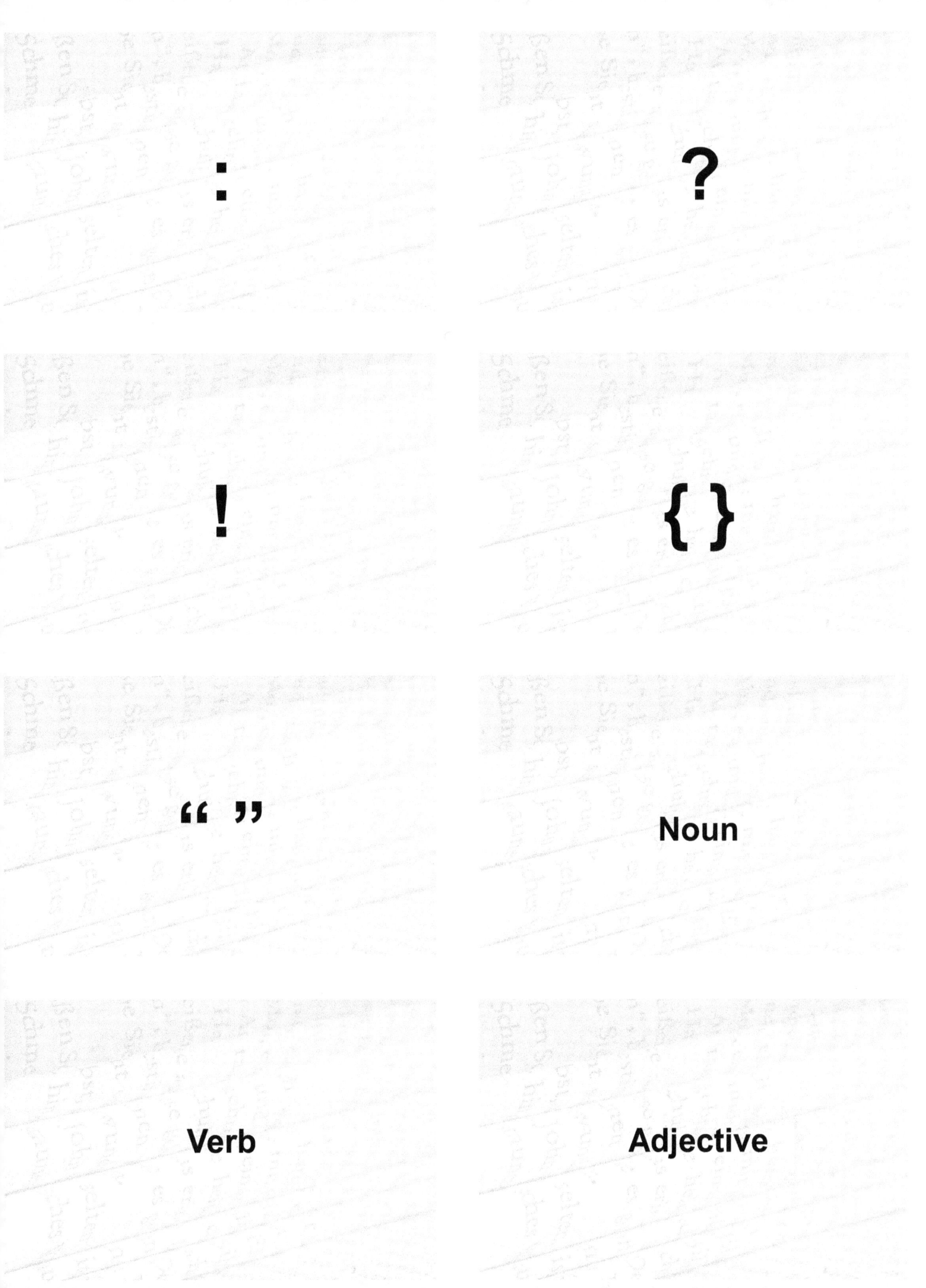

Question Mark	Colon
Ellipses	Exclamation Point
Person, place or thing	Quotation Marks
Modifies a noun	An action

Nominative Case

Objective Case

Possessive Case

Compound Personal Pronouns

Relative Pronouns

Interrogative Pronouns

Indefinite Pronouns

Agreement in Subject and Verb

Me, you, her, him, us, the	I, you, she, he, we, you, they
Myself, yourself, himself, herself, itself, ourselves, yourselves, themselves	My, mine, your, yours, his, her, hers, its, our, ours, their, theirs
Who, which, what	Who, that, which, what
The same in singular or plural form	All, any, both, each, either, everybody, none, one, several, some, someone

Diction Errors

Idiom Errors

Modifiers

Verbs

Base Form of Verbs

Verb Form with -s

Past Tense Verb

Past Participle Verb

Expressions that are not always clear from the meaning of the words (kick the bucket)	Incorrect word choices
Tell what the subject does or what is done to it	Describe words
He/she/it plays	I play
I have played	I played

Present Participle	**Fragment**
Comma Splice	**Run-on Sentence**
Topic Sentence	**Restatement or Restriction**
Illustration	**Analysis**

An incomplete sentence that is punctuated as if it were complete	I am playing
Two independent clauses that are not separated by a conjunction or proper punctuation	Two independent clauses containing a comma
The second sentence can restate or restrict what was written in the first sentence, making the subject more specific	The first sentence introducing the subject of a paragraph
Explain, interpret, and contextualize the illustrations that have been made	This section of the paragraph consists of the illustrations (evidence, data, facts, quotes, ect.) that support your topic

Conclusion	Accept - define
Except - define	Affect (vb.) - define
Effect - define	All right - spelled correctly?
Alright - spelled correctly?	Among

To receive	The final sentence (or two) might review what the paragraph has discussed, and/or reemphasize what is being suggested
To influence, to change	To exclude
Correct spelling	To accomplish (vb.); a result (n.)
When referring to more than two	Incorrect spelling

Between	**Continual**
Continous	**Disinterested**
Uninterested	**Emigrate**
Immigrate	**Eminent**

Recurring actions, repeated regularly and frequently	When referring to only two
Impartial	Occurring without interruption
One emigrates from a place	Not interested
Outstanding, distinguished	One immigrates to a place

Well	Respectfully
Respectively	Set
Sit	Unquestionable
Unquestioned	No exceptions

Courteously	An adverb when referring to how an action is performed
To put or to place	Each in the order given
Indisputable	To be seated
Always, every, all, only, never, none, not, must, necessary	Has not been questioned

Imminent	**Ensure**
Insure	**Farther**
Further	**Fewer**
Less	**Good**

To guarantee; to make safe	Threatening to happen soon
Describes distance	To provide insurance against loss
Used when nouns can be counted and made plural (fewer students)	Additionally; suggests quantity or degree
An adjective before a noun or after a linking verb (look good)	Used when nouns can't be counted or made plural (less homework)

Antecedent	**Denotation**
Connotation	**Transition**
Pronoun	**Conjunction**
Interrogative pronoun	**Fragment**

The literal meaning of a word.	A noun which is referred to using a pronoun.
A way to change to a new topic.	The implied meaning of a word (using context).
A word which is used to connect ideas phrases or sentence parts.	A word which takes the place of a noun (like it or that).
An incomplete sentence.	A pronoun used to start a sentence (who, what, which, whom and whose).

Participle	**5 x 5 essay**
Superscript	**Syntax**
Transition	**Flashback**
Clause	**Phrase**

A five paragraph essay which including an introduction and conclusion paragraph.	A noun which is used as an adjective.
Describes the way words are arranged in a sentence.	A letter or symbol printed above the text line.
When a story shifts to an earlier time.	A sentence or phrase which connects two paragraphs and adds to the coherence.
Part of a sentence which makes some sense but doesn't have a verb or subject.	Part of a sentence containing a subject and predicate.

NOTES

NOTES

NOTES

NOTES

NOTES

NOTES

NOTES

NOTES

www.ingramcontent.com/pod-product-compliance
Lightning Source LLC
Chambersburg PA
CBHW081832300426
44116CB00014B/2563